THE WORLD ECONOMY AT
THE CROSSROADS

THE WORLD ECONOMY
AT THE CROSSROADS

*A Survey of Current Problems of Money, Trade
and Economic Development*

BY

HARRY G. JOHNSON

CLARENDON PRESS . OXFORD

1965

Oxford University Press, Amen House, London, E.C.4.
GLASGOW NEW YORK TORONTO MELBOURNE WELLINGTON
BOMBAY CALCUTTA MADRAS KARACHI LAHORE DACCA
CAPE TOWN SALISBURY NAIROBI IBADAN ACCRA
KUALA LUMPUR HONG KONG

PRINTED IN GREAT BRITAIN BY
DIEMER AND REYNOLDS LTD, BEDFORD.

Preface

THE survey of current problems of international
economic organization presented in this volume
originated as a series of three lectures delivered at
Sir George Williams University, Montreal, at the
beginning of December 1964—the K. E. Norris
Memorial Lectures, sponsored by the Alumni Association of the University. I should like to express my
gratitude to the members of that University, and also
to Mr. Maurice Gold, Chairman of the Alumni
Association, for providing the stimulus to organize
my thinking on this complex series of problems, and
also for the gracious hospitality I enjoyed during my
visit to Montreal. Thanks are also due to Dr. H.
Edward English, Research Director of the Canadian
Trade Committee, and to various members of that
Committee for comments that have improved the
clarity and style of the exposition.

In preparing the survey for publication, I have
taken advantage of the opportunity to bring the
chronicle up to date with respect to developments
early in 1965, and to insert references to some recent
writings by myself and others that explore in more
detail the technical economic issues touched on only
briefly in the survey. Otherwise, the exposition is
substantially as presented in the lectures.

HARRY G. JOHNSON

University of Chicago,
February 1965.

Contents

1. INTRODUCTION 1

2. THEORETICAL AND HISTORICAL BACKGROUND 8

3. INTERNATIONAL MONETARY ORGANIZATION 20

4. INTERNATIONAL TRADING ARRANGEMENTS ... 36

5. PROBLEMS OF DEVELOPING COUNTRIES ... 68

INDEX 101

1. Introduction

THE past two years have been characterized by a great deal of activity in the field of international economic relations. In September 1963 the Board of Directors of the International Monetary Fund, and the representatives of the so-called 'Group of Ten' participants in the General Arrangements to Borrow, inaugurated separately studies into ways of strengthening the international monetary system, studies whose results formed the background of the Annual Meeting of the International Monetary Fund held in Tokyo in September 1964. From March until June of 1964, the United Nations Conference on Trade and Development (UNCTAD)—the first such conference to be convened—was in session in Geneva. And since early 1963 the representatives of the nations belonging to the General Agreement on Tariffs and Trade (GATT) have been carrying on negotiations for the 'Kennedy Round' of bargaining for multilateral tariff reductions, which was formally initiated in November 1964.

What is important about all this activity on the international front is not so much the fact that it has been going on, as the fact that it has emphasized and brought to public view serious and sharp divisions among the major countries or groups of countries in the world economy with respect to the direction in which the present system of international economic organization should evolve. These divisions are based on the dissatisfaction of important members of the

world economy with the present system of international economic organization, and the international
institutions in which that system is incorporated.
The international economic system referred to is,
of course, the system prevailing among the nations
of what is commonly described—with some degree of
euphemism—as the 'free world', and not of the
countries of the Communist *bloc*. The divisions
among these nations imply that the present system of
international economic organization, built with so
much careful thought by the Bretton Woods Agreements, must either evolve in new directions to
accommodate the dissatisfied, or run the risk of disintegration. Since the international institutions under
which the system is organized have in fact been
evolving fairly rapidly in recent years in adaptation
to their changing environment and the changing
demands made upon them, the problem for the future
might perhaps be more accurately described as
whether the emerging dissatisfactions can be
adequately dealt with by further and accelerated
evolution of these institutions, or will require a
radical change in the whole framework of international economic organization. In either case, it is
clear that the international economic system has
arrived at a crossroads; and that which direction it
now takes is a vital matter for the future of the world
economy.

The basic lines of cleavage among the members
of the international system are essentially political,
in the broad sense of the term, and involve a division
into three major groups: the Anglo-Saxon group led

by the United States, the European Common Market countries led by France, and the less-developed countries, led largely by the ideas of one man, Dr. Raúl Prebisch. Dr. Prebisch has dominated the Economic Commission for Latin America for most of the post-war period, held the key post of Secretary-General of UNCTAD, and wrote the basic document for the Conference; and his ideas largely shaped the Conference's proceedings and Final Act. The Conference symbolized and also cemented the emergence of the developing countries—and the change of terminology, from 'underdeveloped' to 'less developed' to 'developing', is itself symbolic—as a new and potentially powerful influence in international economic relations. The emergence of this new influence, in turn, has complicated and exacerbated the cleavages between the other two groups that had already been precipitated by the formation of the Common Market.

Broadly speaking, the Anglo-Saxon group stands for the existing international institutions and system of international economic organization, which are indeed largely of its own creation, and takes the position that any apparent problems can be handled by modification and adjustment of the present framework. The Common Market group, on the other hand, is primarily concerned with building up the Common Market as an economic and political force in world affairs. It tends to regard the present international institutions with suspicion, viewing them as instruments for preserving the political and economic dominance in world affairs of the United States,

or of the United States and United Kingdom combined, and to prefer to meet emerging problems by
superimposing new arrangements in which it has a
controlling influence on top of the existing arrangements, instead of by modification of the latter. This
has been especially so in the sphere of international
monetary organization. There is a rather facile
tendency on the part of the United States to attribute
this, as well as other awkward obstinacies of European
behaviour, to the 'third force' ambitions of General
de Gaulle; but European suspicion of the existing
international institutions has deeper roots in the
experience of the immediate post-war period, when
the United States did call the international tune because it alone was paying the piper. In addition, as
the formation of the Common Market itself bears
witness, the European attitude towards a variety of
important problems in the government of international trade is radically at variance with the Anglo-
Saxon attitude, not only over the central issue of
multilateralism and the most-favoured-nation principle versus preferential trading arrangements, but
also and more fundamentally in taking an essentially
political rather than economic view of the nature of
competition in international trade and of the
objectives of governmental intervention in it.

Again speaking broadly, the less-developed
countries as a collectivity are also suspicious of and
hostile to the present institutions of international
economic organization, but for a rather different
reason. They believe, or like to believe, that these
institutions are instruments designed to foster the

further development of the already-advanced countries and to impede or prevent their own economic development. Especially in Latin America, the International Monetary Fund has frequently appeared as the stern enforcer of orthodoxy in fiscal and monetary policy, and the resolute opponent of the inflationary policies that in many less-developed countries are regarded as the *sine qua non* of rapid economic growth. The World Bank has been persistently criticized for its attachment to specific-purpose commercially sound loans, when what these countries want is general-purpose finance on the easiest possible terms. In the trade field GATT and its principles appear to these countries as an arrangement by which the rich get richer at the expense of the poor: not only does the whole apparatus of bargaining for reciprocal tariff reductions appear unfair—both because they have little trade to bargain with, and because bargaining with it would entail sacrificing the protectionist policies on which they believe their growth depends—but the exemption of agricultural products from GATT rules enables the advanced countries (as the less-developed countries see it) to solve their agricultural problems at the expense of the export earnings of the less-developed countries. Underlying all this aversion to the existing institutions of international economic organization is the strong and highly moralistic conviction that the advanced countries are responsible for their less-developed condition, and owe them redress on a massive scale, this redress to be rendered through the unilateral tender of both unencumbered development assistance and special advantages in international trade. This is a political claim on the advanced countries, and to enforce it the less-developed countries have resorted to the one international institution in which nations appear as political equals rather than as economic unequals, and which they can control by force of numbers, the United Nations.

These, then, are the basic lines of cleavage among the nations of the international economy, which must somehow be resolved in the future evolution—or dissolved in the possible future breakdown—of the international economic order; and they are basically of political origin. The foregoing description of them is intended, of course, to be only the briefest of thumbnail sketches; it has necessarily glossed over important divergences of opinion among the members of the various groups—for example, between the United States on the one hand and the United Kingdom or Canada on the other, between France and Italy on the one hand and Germany and the Benelux countries on the other, and among the less-developed countries between net-exporters and net-importers of foodstuffs. Even so, it has been necessary to define these lines of cleavage in terms of specific, and in some cases rather narrowly technical, issues, a fuller explanation of which will be provided subsequently.

The purpose of this survey is to present an exposition and explanation of the major outstanding issues of international economic organization. The exposition begins with a general discussion of the importance of a liberal system of international trade, payments, and capital movements for world prosperity and economic growth, and a brief account of the development of international economic organization and institutions up to the immediate post-war period. This theory and history provides an introduction to and background for a more detailed examination of the three major problem areas of contemporary international economic relations, namely international monetary organization, international trading arrangements, and the special problems of developing countries, to each of which a section of the survey is assigned.

2. Theoretical and Historical Background

THE desirability of a liberal system of international trade has been a commonplace of economic discourse ever since the classical economists produced the principle of comparative advantage. According to that principle, freedom of trade permits each country to specialize on the production of those goods which it can produce most efficiently, and to avoid wasting resources on producing goods that it can produce only inefficiently, instead importing such goods from countries that can produce them more efficiently and paying for them by exports of the goods that it can produce efficiently. Thus freedom of trade promotes maximum efficiency of utilization of the world's human, material, and natural resources. By an extension of the logic of this analysis, which the classical economists were prevented from making by their assumption of immobility of labour between countries, but which their successors find it natural to make, maximum efficiency of utilization of resources is also promoted by freedom of international movement of labour and capital—freedom of migration and international investment—since self-interest will prompt individuals to move themselves or their capital from locations where their services make a relatively small contribution to production, and therefore have a low value, to locations where their services make a relatively larger contribution to production, and therefore have a higher value.

Recognition of the desirability of a well-functioning

international monetary system, and definition of what 'well-functioning' implies, is of much more recent origin. The recognition dates from the disruption of the nineteenth-century gold standard system by the First World War, and the international monetary difficulties and breakdown of the inter-war period; and it derives primarily from the emergence of price stability and the maintenance of satisfactory levels of employment as objectives of national economic policy. To be consistent with the pursuit and satisfactory achievement of these objectives— the importance of which for prosperity and economic welfare does not require elaboration—the international monetary system must provide some combination of international liquidity (international reserves and credit facilities) and international adjustment mechanisms adequate to permit the financing of transitory balance-of-payments deficits, and the rectification of more fundamental balance-of-payments disequilibria, without requiring the countries involved to pursue sharply deflationary or inflationary policies; or alternatively to resort to the imposition or variation of barriers to international trade and capital movements. A mal-functioning international monetary system, in other words, leads to inefficiency and waste, either directly, through obliging countries to undergo unemployment of their productive facilities or the distorting influences of inflation; or indirectly, through forcing them to resort to interventions in trade and payments that reduce the efficiency of resource allocation in their own economies and in the

B

international system as a whole. A further important characteristic of a well-functioning international monetary system is that it must not lend itself to being an independent source of international disturbance, by promoting speculative movements of capital from country to country.

The description of the advantages of a liberal international economic order just outlined is expressed in what economists refer to as 'static terms', that is, it refers to the efficiency of utilization of the stocks of productive resources existing at a particular point of time. It has always been fashionable—and is at present extremely fashionable—among the spokesmen for the poorer and less-developed countries of the world—the United States, Germany, and others in the nineteenth century; the new nations of the present time—to deride these arguments for a liberal international system as 'static', and to assert that when 'dynamic' considerations of economic growth and development are taken into account everything somehow becomes different, and economic analysis must be stood on its head; liberal international economic policies being held responsible for the condition of economic backwardness, and anti-liberal policies being recommended as sure-fire remedies for that condition. On the contrary, the argument for a liberal international economic order in the dynamic context of growth and development is far stronger than it is in the static context of efficiency; and it is the pursuit of illiberal economic policies—by both advanced and less-developed countries—rather than the pursuit of liberal economic policies that constitutes a major impediment to the development of the less-developed countries.

The logic of this point of view may best be conveyed by sketching out a theoretical model of the process of economic development as it would occur in a freely competitive world economy. Economic development may be defined in a very broad sense as the process of raising income per head through the accumulation of capital, where the concept of capital includes not merely material capital or wealth but human capital in the form of trained and skilled workers, managers, and professional people, and intellectual capital in the form of scientific knowledge. The accumulation of capital occurs in consequence of profitable opportunities for investment of resources in the creation of capital of these different types, and is subject to economies of scale because the resulting growth of income enlarges the market, and therefore the opportunities for specialization and division of labour in the application of human and non-human capital and the application of science. For this reason, and also because increasing income increases the capacity to accumulate capital, economic development in a particular part of the world will have a self-reinforcing and agglomerating quality about it. This quality is thoroughly familiar to students of economic development, and is expressed in such concepts as Rostow's 'take-off', Myrdal's 'cumulative circular causation', and Perroux's 'pôles de croissance'. What needs to be emphasized, however, is that in a freely competitive world the process of economic development would inevitably tend to spread out from the country or region of origin to the rest of the world, as a consequence of the pursuit of private profit. The spread of the process of development would result primarily from two mechanisms called into operation by economic development itself. One is the growing pressure of demand on natural resources, which would promote exploration for and exploitation of new sources of supply, and the development of other parts of the world possessing such resources with the aid of capital, technology, and trained labour supplied by the developing centre. The other is the pressure of demand on available labour, and the effects of economic development in raising the real wages of labour in the developing region, relative to real wages in the rest of the world. The availability of higher wages in the developing centre would tend to attract immigration of labour from the outside; more important, the availability of low-wage labour in the rest of the world would promote emigration of capital and technology to take advantage of it in competing for sales in the market of the developing centre. In addition, since forgone real wages are the largest component of the alternative-opportunity cost of investing in education and training, there would be a growing incentive to train up the labour of the low-wage areas to the skills possessed in the advanced areas. The operation of these mechanisms would in turn lay the foundations on which the rest of the world could join in the self-reinforcing process of development.

It is important to note that these mechanisms for the diffusion of economic growth depend on freedom of international competition, inasmuch as their operation presupposes freedom of access to the markets of the developing centre. They will be impeded to the extent that the centre seeks to prevent the transfer of production to lower-cost external sources by protection and other means. Unfortunately, the centre will automatically be under pressure to do so, since the rise in wages that goes with economic development will put competitive pressure on those industries and activities that have difficulty in off-setting rising labour costs by substituting capital equipment for labour and improving their technology, and these industries, in part because they are labour-intensive, will have the political power to demand protection. The pressure for protective policies will depend also on the mobility of labour and capital among occupations; a major reason why advanced countries typically give heavy protection to their agriculture is the immobility of labour off the land, and the immobility of agricultural land into other profitable uses. Protectionism in the less-developed regions, on the other hand, may conceivably accelerate the transmission of the development process. The infant industry argument for protection asserts that it will, but experience suggests that its effect is generally to impede development by establishing a high-cost inefficient industrial structure parasitic on the country's export activities or on its general economic system.

Finally, it should be noted that the efficiency and speed of the growth-transmitting mechanisms depend intimately on the dynamic efficiency of the international monetary system. If the international monetary system provides a growing stock of liquidity sufficient to permit the advanced countries to maintain full employment and grow steadily, and includes methods for smooth adjustment of balance-of-payments disequilibria, the growth-transmitting mechanisms will work efficiently, and it will be in the economic interests of the advanced countries to have them operating. If, on the other hand, the international monetary system works poorly, and particularly if it imposes chronic deflationary pressure on the world economy, the advanced countries will have an incentive to resist the operation of these mechanisms in the interests of maintaining their domestic employment and balancing their international accounts.

These theoretical considerations provide a background for a necessarily brief sketch of the evolution of international economic organization up to the beginning of the contemporary period. In the nineteenth century the world economy was centred on Britain, the pioneer of the Industrial Revolution. While Britain had abundant coal and iron resources to support her manufacturing, her available agricultural land was limited; and her manufacturing supremacy, together with the growing pressure of her population on the land, led her to adopt a policy of free trade. This policy was ideal for Britain's own economic development; but it also ensured that the process of economic development was transmitted to the rest of the world through the investment of British capital and the migration of British people to develop the external supplies of foodstuffs and raw materials that Britain's industrial growth increasingly demanded. The development of natural resources in the 'regions of recent settlement', as they are frequently called—North and South America, Australia-New Zealand, and South Africa—was complementary to British economic growth, but laid the foundations for subsequent industrial growth in these regions. Britain's central position in the world economy as leading manufacturer, exporter of manufactures and importer of foodstuffs and materials, and supplier of capital for the finance of world trade and development investment, also meant that the international monetary system, though increasingly a gold standard system in form, was essentially a sterling standard system, controlled by the Bank of England. The system functioned smoothly for this reason, and also because Britain's central position was built on its role as a discount and acceptance centre, which meant that Britain was a short-term creditor *vis-à-vis* the other nations, so that Bank of England policy operated by varying the amount of short-term foreign lending by the British capital market. (In contrast, the key currency countries of the modern world have been deposit centres— short-term debtors to other countries—so that their monetary and other policies must operate by varying the amount of short-term lending by foreigners they attract; this involves a dependence on the confidence of domestic and foreign owners of short-term capital, and a vulnerability to speculative capital movements, that does not exist for a discount and acceptance centre.)

The process of complementary development of the world economy, centred on Britain's leadership in manufacturing and deriving from Britain's lack of agricultural resources, was already disintegrating in the latter nineteenth century, with the deceleration of British industrial growth after about 1870, and the industrial development—fostered or perhaps merely accompanied by protectionist policies—of countries with more abundant natural resources, notably the United States, Germany, and France. But the international system proved capable of absorbing these structural changes—which occurred gradually—until it was abruptly shattered by the outbreak and consequences of the First World War.

There is much truth in the claim that war is the ultimate experience of, and justification for, protection; and the First World War left a heavy legacy of increased protection. Not only did protection of industrial products increase—even Britain made a major breach in its traditional policy of free trade, largely on the grounds of defence considerations—but the European countries took steps to protect their farmers against the competition of cheap grains from North and South America, Australia, and South Africa, in large part to maintain their supply of soldiers for future wars. In addition the United States, which emerged from the War in the position of industrial leader that Britain had previously occupied, and should have been moving towards freer trade, adopted in the Smoot-Hawley tariff of 1930 a much more strongly protectionist policy than it had previously practised. Increased protectionism was also apparent in a tightening of immigration legislation, especially in the United States, which raised the barriers to the international mobility of human beings.

Far more serious for the world economy than the rise of protectionism was the failure to re-establish a stable international monetary system. It was attempted to re-establish the pre-war gold standard; but in the event the pound was over-valued and the franc under-valued; and the post-war extension of the gold standard to many more countries than had previously been on it gave rise to a demand for gold greater than the available stocks, which was satisfied temporarily by the development of the gold exchange standard. The overvaluation of the pound made Britain chronically depressed and economically stagnant, with a serious retarding effect on economic growth elsewhere; it also made the preservation of the value of sterling dependent on commanding sufficient foreign deposits. And Britain was no longer the unique centre of the international financial and monetary system; the system was now multi-centred, with the United States newly emerged as a major banking centre and source of capital for international lending. It was a shaky system, dependent on widespread holding of national currencies as a substitute for non-existent gold, and hence vulnerable to speculative international movements of capital; and it had to survive in a world fraught with national and international political tensions. It was set up and kept functioning in the 1920's by collaboration between the world's two strongest central banks, the Bank of England and the Federal Reserve; but central bank collaboration was insufficient to prevent it from collapsing like a house of cards in 1931, under the strains produced by the Great Crash. In the wake of its collapse—and of the Great Depression itself— came a period of severe monetary disorganization, from which countries attempted to rescue themselves at each other's expense by resort to greatly increased protection, combined with preferential and bilateral trading arrangements. The result was a violent constriction of the volume and choking-up of the channels of international trade.

It was from the lessons of the experience of the 1930's that the world's leading international economic experts derived the fundamental ideas they applied in devising international institutions for the reconstruction of the international economy after the Second World War. These institutions were to be three in number: (1) an International Monetary Fund, to supplement the world's inadequate gold supply by credit facilities and in various ways to promote orderly adjustment of balance-of-payments disequilibria; (2) an International Trade Organization (whose function has instead been assumed by the General Agreement on Tariffs and Trade) to ensure non-discriminatory practices in commercial policy and to serve as an agency for negotiating the liberalization of trade; and (3) an International Bank for Reconstruction and Development (now known as 'the World Bank') to channel long-term capital to international investment in a steadier and more regular flow than private capital markets had previously provided. All three were designed to remedy specific defects of the preceding system of international economic organization as they appeared from the experience of the 1930's; and for that very reason all three have been imperfectly adapted to the emerging problems of the post-war world, have had to be adapted in face of these problems, and are faced with the necessity of evolving still further if they are to continue to be useful. The major problems referred to are, as previously mentioned, connected with the evolution of relations between Europe and the United States and with the growth in international political importance of the less-developed countries.

3. International Monetary Organisation

THE International Monetary Fund was constructed with four specific problems of the 1930's very much in mind. In the first place, the collapse of the gold exchange standard had revealed the weakness of a system in which a shortage of monetary gold was made good by substituting holdings of national currencies convertible into gold, or reliance on negotiation of borrowings of reserves from other countries. The IMF was therefore designed to provide a stock of international credit facilities that could be drawn on by members in balance-of-payments deficit. The specific plan adopted involves members contributing a quota to the Fund, of which 25 per cent. is in gold and 75 per cent. in the member's own currency; in return they can borrow other members' currencies by purchasing them from the Fund, up to the limit of a Fund holding of their currency equal to 200 per cent. of their quota, these purchases being subject to increasing restrictive terms and conditions as the percentage of currency quota held by the Fund rises. It should be noted that the 'currency fund' device has two built-in features that can be (and have been) sources of difficulty in its operation. One is that the Fund may not contain a sufficient stock of the currency or currencies that a member wishes to borrow. The other is that an increase in the size of the Fund, designed to provide more liquidity, requires additional subscriptions of gold, and to obtain the requisite gold members may resort to converting their holdings of other members' currencies into gold, thus aggravating the balance-of-payments problems of the others.

Secondly, the experience of the collapse of the gold exchange standard and its aftermath had shown that, while exchange rate changes were necessary to remedy fundamental disequilibrium, such changes could not be left to the free decisions of national authorities, both because countries might resort to 'offensive' devaluation as a substitute for appropriate domestic expansionary policies, and because countries could cancel out each others' exchange rate changes. The International Monetary Fund was therefore designed to be an institution through which internationally agreed changes in particular exchange rates could be implemented, when such change were necessitated by 'fundamental disequilibrium'. Thirdly, since movements of 'hot money' from country to country had been a major initiating factor in the 1930's collapse and subsequent disturbances, the rules of the IMF allowed countries to exercise control over short-term capital movements. Finally, since it was generally agreed that a major defect of the gold standard system was its 'deflationary bias'—due to the fact that while the efflux of reserves put pressure on the deficit country to remedy its deficit, the influx of reserves put no such pressure on the surplus country to remedy its surplus—the Articles of Agreement of the IMF included a 'scarce currency cause' permitting members to discriminate in their commercial policies against any member whose currency became scarce in the Fund. This clause was more or less explicitly designed for use against the United States, whose propensity to accumulate gold in the inter-war period, and especially in the latter 1930's, was widely held to have been responsible for the inter-war difficulties and was expected to continue to present a problem in the future.

The IMF was therefore designed to start the post-war world off with an international monetary system free of the defects of the previous system. But both defects in its design—particularly, the small size of the initial Fund and the erroneous basic assumption that all currencies can be treated as equal in international trade and payments—and the nature and magnitude of the immediate post-war monetary disequilibrium problem conspired to set the Fund outside the main stream of developments. The immediate post-war problem was the reconstruction and economic recovery of the European countries, which required large-scale assistance from the only area capable of supplying the necessary real resources, North America; on the monetary side this problem appeared as the problem of 'dollar shortage'. The real resources needed were beyond the capacity of Europe's own financial resources and those of the Fund to supply; instead, the dollars were supplied directly by the United States under the Marshall Plan; and, as a logical corollary, use of the Fund by the European countries was suspended during the period of the Marshall Plan. The isolation of the Fund from European developments during those years had important implications for the future: In the first place, various incidents in 1947-9 fostered the feeling in Europe that the Fund was an American policy instrument, at a time when Europe was peculiarly sensitive about American domination. Secondly, largely as a consequence of the form in which Marshall Aid was given—in dollars to finance dollar balance-of-payments deficits, with the corresponding real resources having to be reallocated among countries according to their recovery requirements—the European countries had to develop their own institutions of international monetary co-operation on a regional basis—the successive Intra-European Payments Schemes and the European Payments Union, which after the end of the Marshall Plan became the European Monetary Agreement. Thus there became established a tradition of European monetary co-operation, outside of and apart from the IMF.

Meanwhile, the dominating position in world trade, payments, and capital movements that the United States had perforce assumed was rapidly fostering another development that by-passed the IMF system—the growth in use of the U.S. dollar as an international reserve currency, in substitution for the use of gold. The growing use of the dollar as an international reserve currency, together with the gradual transfer of gold reserves from the United States to other, mainly European, countries that accompanied it, played an important part in permitting the rapid post-war expansion in international trade and payments. This would otherwise have been constricted by a growing shortage of monetary gold, since current new supplies of monetary gold (the excess of new production over hoarding, which has been substantial) have not added to monetary gold stocks as rapidly as the demand for international reserves has grown. On the other hand, the emergence of the dollar as an international reserve currency has re-created the gold exchange standard of the 1920's, which broke down so disastrously in the 1930's, with all its inherent problems. These problems began to appear very rapidly after 1957, when, as a result of European economic recovery, the delayed effects of the 1949 European devaluations, and to some extent of domestic inflation and its own foreign military and economic assistance programmes, the United States balance of payments moved into chronic and substantial deficit. They have been aggravated by the return of the European currencies to convertibility at the end of 1958, which has provided an international environment conducive to the international mobility of capital, and by strong resistance on the part of the monetary authorities and governments of the major countries to exchange rate changes as a means of correcting international disequilibria. On the United States side, that resistance is associated with the obligation not to devalue that a reserve currency country is assumed to have towards its creditors. On the European side, it is associated with the experience of the 1949 devaluations, which by hindsight appear to have been unnecessarily harsh and disturbing, and especially with the notion, emphasized by the Americans at that time, that deficits are a consequence of inflationary sins that must be atoned for by devaluation in the deficit country, not condoned by appreciation in the surplus country. The result has been that the present international monetary system has become a system of rigid exchange rates like the old gold standard, contrary to the intentions of the planners of the IMF; further contrary to the assumption of the planners, it has proved impossible (or, at least, inexpedient) to devise effective controls over short-term capital movements, which have returned to plague the stability of the system.

What are the major defects of a system of fixed exchange rates based on gold but entailing large-scale holdings of national currencies as international reserves in substitution for gold? International monetary experts have come to distinguish three major problems that characterize such a system—the confidence problem, the long-run liquidity problem, and the adjustment problem.[1]

The confidence problem is concerned with the danger that a loss of confidence in one of the reserve currencies—or a gain in confidence in another—will lead to massive conversions of funds out of or into a particular currency, precipitating demands for gold that cannot be met (since the gold backing of the reserve currencies is inadequate), and so bringing about a collapse of the system in a scramble for non-existent gold through the liquidation of reserve currency holdings. It is important to note that since

1. See Fritz Machlup and Burton G. Malkiel (eds.), *International Monetary Arrangements: The Problem of Choice*, report on the deliberations of an international study group of 32 economists (Princeton, N.J.: Princeton University Press, 1964).

only central banks are entitled to convert currencies into gold, such a collapse could only occur as a result of central bank actions, so that the confidence problem is a matter of central banks' confidence in each other's country's economic policies; this feature, besides putting possible conflicts of national interest at the centre of operation of the system, gives altogether undue power to central bankers in the operation of the international economic system.

The long-run liquidity problem is as follows: if total international reserves are to grow faster than basic reserves in the form of gold, holdings of reserve currencies must grow faster than the gold reserves backing them; so that the liquidity position—ratio of gold reserves to short-term liabilities to foreign countries—of the reserve-currency country or countries must deteriorate over time; further, the reserve currency country can only supply additional reserves to other countries by running a continuous deficit on its balance of payments. Both the deficit and the deterioration of the liquidity position sap the confidence in the reserve currency on which its use as a substitute reserve depends; thus the system contains an internal contradiction, which can only be corrected either by voluntary agreement by other countries to tolerate the deficit and steadily reduce their holdings of gold relative to reserve currencies, or by provision of a supplement to gold other than national currencies. In addition, the system makes the long-run growth of reserves depend on the vagaries of new gold production and hoarding, the balance-of-payments experience of the reserve-currency countries, and whatever *ad hoc* arrangements are made from time to time to supplement the gold and national currency reserves with international credit facilities.

The adjustment problem derives from the consideration that the function of international liquidity is to finance deficits that are in process of being corrected, not to remove the need for correction, and is concerned with what mechanisms the system provides for bringing about adjustment. Adjustment is fundamentally a problem of the international realignment of prices and costs. A fixed exchange rate system rules out one mechanism for accomplishing such realignment, changes in exchange rates. The objectives of price stability, high employment, and economic growth adopted by modern economic policy rule out the major mechanism relied on under the old gold standard, deflation in deficit countries and inflation in surplus countries. Adjustment in the present system has therefore come to depend on two other mechanisms: the use of interventions in trade and payments on an *ad hoc* temporary basis, to secure improvement in the balance of payments in the short run—which is not 'adjustment' in the fundamental sense but a means of averting the consequences of non-adjustment—and reliance on the inability of governments to achieve the objectives of price stability and full employment in the face of sustained balance-of-payments pressures to the contrary, a reliance reinforced by resort to inter-governmental lecturing on the subject of the responsibilities of deficit and surplus countries to the system.

These problems have, as already mentioned, become acute since the emergence of the United States as a chronic deficit country after 1957. So far as the confidence and long-run liquidity problems are concerned, there have been two alternative practical lines of development to follow—to strengthen the reserve currency system built on the U.S. dollar, and to strengthen and increase the role of the International Monetary Fund in the international monetary system.

To describe these as the practical alternatives is, of course, to exclude two proposals that have been strongly advocated by some academic experts in recent years—to return to the gold standard by means of a sufficient increase in the price of gold and subsequent adherence to the gold standard rules of the game, and to replace the present system by a system of freely floating exchange rates. Both proposals seek to replace the discretionary management of the present arrangements by an automatic self-regulatory system, the difference between them being that gold-standard proponents seek to subject national monetary authorities to international discipline, whereas floating-rate proponents seek to free national monetary authorities from such discipline—if one distrusts one's own government one favours the gold standard, if one distrusts other countries' governments one favours floating exchange rates.

Up to the middle of 1963 the main line of evolution in the international monetary system lay along the route of strengthening the reserve currency system rather than the Fund. The potential role of the Fund was indeed strengthened by an increase in quotas agreed in 1958, by its own development of the technique of 'stand-by' credit facilities for countries in balance-of-payments difficulties, and by the General Arrangements to Borrow agreed on in 1961-2. These Arangements ensured the Fund an adequate supply of the major European currencies, thereby overcoming the defect of the quota system mentioned earlier, that the Fund may lack a sufficient stock of currencies a member in deficit desires to purchase; but the terms on which the Arrangements to Borrow can be invoked vest discretionary power over the availability of the currencies in the countries supplying them, reflecting the interest of the European countries in keeping control in their own hands and out of the IMF's. The main line of evolution, however, lay outside the Fund, a consequence on the one hand of the stance taken by U.S. policy towards the deficit—which was largely shaped by Mr. Robert V. Roosa during his period as Under Secretary for Monetary Affairs in the United States Treasury—and on the other of the attitudes towards, and suspicions of, the United States and the IMF on the part of the European countries. Until 1963 the United States consistently took the view that its deficit was temporary and due soon to disappear, that the dollar was fundamentally sound, and that it was the obligation of other countries to assist in supporting it through a period of difficulty always expected to be short. Accordingly, the United States, at the instigation and with the active participation of Mr. Roosa, became involved in a succession of *ad hoc* arrangements with various European countries—currency swaps, pre-

payments of past loans, the issuance of medium-
term securities denominated in foreign currencies—
designed to improve the appearance of the U.S.
balance of payments and finance it without serious
loss of gold. The European partners to these arrangements joined in them partly out of growing recognition that they were in fact obliged to do so to keep
the international monetary system functioning, partly
out of appreciation of the political leverage they
acquired thereby over the United States.

In the late summer of 1963, however, the United
States changed its position, presumably because the
opportunities for further *ad hoc* arrangements had
reached the point of exhaustion and because new
evidence indicated that the U.S. deficit was likely to
continue for some years. The European countries
had also been becoming restive about the amounts of
credit they had supplied to the United States, and
about some of the implications of recent *ad hoc*
arrangements. A Study Group of representatives of
the ten participants in the General Arrangements to
Borrow was set up to review the functioning of the
international monetary system and its probable
future needs for liquidity. A parallel study was con-
ducted by the IMF; the findings of both were published in time for discussion at the September 1964
annual meeting of the IMF.

The important document here is the *Ministerial
Statement* of the Group of Ten, and its *Annex* prepared by Deputies.[2] Its importance lies as much in
the issues it leaves open as in those it settles. Not un-
expectedly, the Statement affirms the adequacy of the

present system of fixed exchange rates based on the present price of gold; where it makes a new departure is in admitting the possibility of a future need for new international reserve assets, and setting up a further study group to examine this question. In this connection the Statement supports a 'moderate' increase in Fund quotas, combined with some adjustment of individual country quotas to align them with the relevant countries' importance in world trade—such an increase, in the order of 25 per cent., has been set in train by the IMF, and great care has been taken to avoid creating problems for the U.S. by inducing conversions of dollars into gold for subscription of the gold portion of the quota increase. The strains that have arisen in the operation of the international monetary system in recent years are reflected in the Statement—in the emphasis given on the one hand to problems of adjustment, which are to be subjected to further study; and on the other to new arrangements for something called 'multilateral surveillance' of ways and means of financing payments disequilibria (a term obviously chosen to paper-over disagreement about the extent to which third parties should have a voice in bilateral credit arrangements of the type that have become common in recent years).

In terms of the three problems of the present international monetary system outlined earlier, the strengthening of international monetary co-operation

2. *Ministerial Statement* of the Group of Ten and *Annex* prepared by Deputies, reprinted in *Federal Reserve Bulletin*, 50, no. 11 (August 1964), 975-99; see also *International Monetary Fund, 1964 Annual Report*, Part II (Washington, D.C., 1964).

evident on and under the surface of the developments
of 1963-4 clearly implies that the confidence problem
has been resolved, though some residual areas have
been left for bickering among central banks. This fact
was indeed impressively demonstrated by the prompt-
ness and adequacy with which international financial
support was provided for the pound sterling in the
balance-of-payments crisis of late 1964. There remain,
however, the long-run liquidity problem and the
adjustment problem. These problems, and especially
the adjustment problem, have become more urgent
in consequence of the sharp deterioration of the
United States deficit in the last quarter of 1964, and
the increasing impatience of the European surplus
countries with the balance-of-payments performance
of the United States, expressed most dramatically in
General de Gaulle's attack on the present international
monetary system and demand for a return to the gold
standard in his speech of early February 1965.

As regards the long-run liquidity problem, the
recognition by the Group of Ten of the existence of
such a problem is at least encouraging; but the real
question is how much will be done about it and in
what way. The Ministerial Statement leaves open
the question whether the new reserve asset envisaged
should be provided through the IMF or outside it;
and the Group's support for the enlargement of
Fund quotas agreed on in September 1964 was
clearly intended not to pre-judge that question, nor
will the increase in quotas do more than preserve
the *status quo ante* recent developments. According
to all indications, the Europeans would much prefer

future increases in liquidity to be provided outside the IMF, through implementation of the Bernstein multiple-reserve-currency plan.[3] Under this plan, new reserve assets would be provided in the form of bundles of national currencies combined in fixed ratios, which countries would be obliged to hold within a margin of ratios to their gold holdings. The plan has the attraction of building on and stabilizing the reserve currency system by spreading the reserve currency role among the major national currencies; but one suspects that its chief attraction to the European countries is that it will give them control over the amount of the new reserve asset to be created, control which will enable them to resist what they regard as the inflationary influence of the United States. (This question of the alleged inflationary impact of the United States deficit has been a source of much confusion and misunderstanding between Europe and the United States; the Americans argue that American prices have been relatively stable, and that the United States current account has shown a large surplus, so that, if anything, the United States has exercised a deflationary influence; what the Europeans mean is that financing the over-all deficit of the United States has faced them with problems of unwanted monetary expansion.) This motivation gives reason for fear that the adoption of the multiple-

3. The Bernstein plan, originated by Dr. Edward F. Bernstein, former Research Director of the IMF, has been circulated privately but not published in an easily accessible source.
   For details of other plans advanced in recent years, see Herbert G. Grubel, *World Monetary Reform: Plans and Issues* (Stanford: Stanford University Press, 1963).

currency-reserve plan would exercise a deflationary drag on the growth of world trade and payments. From the point of view of ensuring growth of international liquidity at a rate sufficient to support stable growth of world trade and payments, a preferable solution would be for holdings of currency reserves to be centralized and internationalized through transformation of the IMF into a world central bank, with powers to govern the aggregate growth of international reserves through appropriate open market operations, on the plan propounded on various occasions by Professor Robert Triffin of Yale University.[4]

Finally, as regards the adjustment problem, it has already been mentioned that adjustment under the present system is a matter of *ad hoc* interventions in trade and payments designed to disguise disequilibrium, coupled with dependence on the passage of time in disequilibrium conditions to bring about genuine adjustment, contrary to the other policy objectives of the countries concerned. There is, indeed, a strong prevailing tendency to gloss over the difference between spurious and genuine adjustment, and in so doing to sanction the use of interventions in trade and payments to preserve the appearance

4. The main outlines of the Triffin plan are presented in Robert Triffin, *Gold and the Dollar Crisis* (New Haven: Yale University Press, 1960), though the details have been modified in Professor Triffin's numerous subsequent writings on the subject.

For discussion of the proposal for a world central bank, see Harry G. Johnson, "International Liquidity—Problems and Plans", *Malayan Economic Review*, VIII, no. 1 (April 1962), 1-19, reprinted in Grubel, op. cit., 369-91, and Harry G. Johnson, *The Canadian Quandary* (Toronto: McGraw-Hill of Canada, 1963), 297-322.

of balance-of-payments equilibrium. To do so is to
lose sight of the ultimate purposes of international
monetary organization in the pursuit of a functioning
international monetary system. The ultimate purpose
of the international monetary system is to facilitate
freedom of competition in trade and payments, and
to free international transactions from arbitrary interventions prompted by monetary developments
themselves. When freedom of international competition becomes subservient to the maintenance of
a particular set of exchange rates, as it has increasingly done in recent years, means have changed
places with ends. It may be suggested that the trend
towards the use of interventions for balance-of-
payments purposes calls for re-thinking of the monetary system itself. Under the present system,
adjustment occurs by natural competitive realignment of prices and costs, so slowly that the resultant
deficits are too large to be manageable under existing
international monetary arrangements, and have to
be handled by what Roosa has termed 'systematic
ad-hoc-ery'. One alternative would be to recognize
that payments imbalances are of this magnitude, and
to seek to finance them not by banking credits but
by long-term intergovernmental loans (and possibly
grants) following the precedents of war finance, the
Marshall Plan, and development assistance. Another
would be to revive and make use of the machinery
for changing exchange rates in cases of fundamental
disequilibrium, which the International Monetary
Fund was intended to provide but which has been
allowed to fall into disuse.

4. International Trading Arrangements

THE preceding section of this survey traced the evolution of the new post-war institution designed to establish a better-functioning international monetary system, the International Monetary Fund; described how it had been shunted from the centre of the picture by the post-war dollar shortage problem and the growth of the use of the dollar as an international reserve currency; and posed the two outstanding problems of international monetary organization that remain to be resolved. These are: whether the long-run liquidity needs of the international economy are to be provided by a rational centralization of reserve-holding and reserve-creation in an International Monetary Fund transformed into a world central bank, or are to be left to *ad hoc* extension of the gold exchange standard by reluctant co-operation among the leading nations and their central banks; and whether effective mechanisms of financing and especially of adjusting balance-of-payments disequilibria will be worked out, or the international economy will continue to rely on *ad hoc* policies whose function is more often to conceal than to heal balance-of-payments ailments. This section examines in the same fashion the evolution of the institution designed to reconstruct a liberal system of international trade—the proposed International Trade Organization, set up by the Havana Charter, the failure of which to win ratification in the United States Senate led to the assumption of the same responsibilities by the General Agreement on Tariffs and Trade. The section begins with a description of the conditions the institution was designed to correct, and outlines its main provisions and their shortcomings; it then recounts the relevant aspects of the post-war evolution of the world economy, and states and comments on the problems outstanding at present.

The brief account of the development of the world economy and of international economic organization up to the collapse of the 1930's provided in Section II mentioned, in addition to the adoption by Britain of a policy of free trade, the fact that other nations in the nineteenth century attempted to foster their own industrial growth by policies of protection, and that protectionism increased after the First World War. In order to appreciate the character of the disorganization of trade in the chaotic conditions of the 1930's, and therefore the problems the post-war planners sought to remedy and their ideas of how to do so, it is necessary first to understand the essential principles of the international conventions governing the commercial policies of nations that had emerged from historical experience. The basic principles were, first, that governmental intervention in trade should take the form of the imposition of tariffs, the point being that a tariff constitutes a known and constant barrier that it is possible for a foreign producer to overcome if he is competitive enough; and second, that government intervention in trade should be non-discriminatory as between foreign nations, exception being allowed for the relation between an imperial power and its dependencies. This principle was embodied in the use of the most-favoured-nation clause in commercial treaties between states, according to which a signatory country obliges itself to give its co-signatory partner as favourable treatment in international commercial dealings as it gives to other countries with which it signs commercial treaties. In its origins, this clause was a means of guaranteeing good faith in commercial negotiations, by preventing the signatories to treaties from rendering concessions given to one another nugatory by giving still more favourable concessions to countries not party to the original agreement. But it gradually became—especially in American thinking, where it dovetailed neatly with other idealistic equalitarian ideas on the nature of states and the proper relations between them—a canon of fair practice in commercial policy towards other states.

This structure of international conventions shattered under the pressure of the Great Depression and its aftermath. An early development was the establishment of British Imperial Preference, which was largely designed to soften the blow on fellow Commonwealth members of the protectionism to which each member resorted in the face of the Depression, and which irritated the United States—for fairly self-evident historical reasons—so greatly as to become a prime target of subsequent U.S. foreign economic policy, with consequences that were expressed concretely in the emphasis placed on the principle of non-discrimination in the ITO Charter and GATT.

But much worse was to come: under the pressure

of balance-of-payments deficits induced by the collapse of commodity prices and employment and the scramble for gold, countries resorted to import quotas, exchange controls, and other non-tariff barriers to trade (such as over-valuation for customs purposes, administrative delays and difficulties, and the enforcement of labelling and health requirements) to restrict their imports and protect their international reserves and domestic employment. These devices had the two great advantages over tariff increases of being certain to restrict the country's imports—whereas tariff increases could be offset by sufficient reductions in the prices charged by foreign suppliers—and of not explicitly abrogating existing tariff agreements with the country's trading partners. Resort to them, however, though apparently efficacious and necessary to each individual country, was bound to be mutually self-defeating for all countries taken together, and to result chiefly in greatly worsening the international allocation of resources and seriously impairing the efficiency of what production was carried on.

Very soon countries short of international reserves realized that some part at least of these adverse effects could be avoided by resorting to bilateral trading agreements and clearing arrangements, under which trade in both directions with a partner country could be expanded without risk of loss of reserves. Given the initial situation of fixed exchange rates, lack of international reserves, excess capacity in most lines of production, and severe all-round restrictions on international trade imposed for balance-of-payments

reasons, such devices could produce a genuine and
mutually beneficial improvement in the situation
without really harming third countries—this was indeed subsequently recognized in the dollar-shortage
period, when such devices were again resorted to. But
at the time, and especially to the United States,
which, as a country that had depreciated its currency
early and was enjoying a vast gold inflow, had no
comprehension of the forces controlling policy in
other countries, the resort to bilateralism appeared
merely as brazen discrimination against third parties and a violation of their legitimate rights.
Bilateralism acquired additional ill repute by being
used by the Nazis as a means of exploiting their
neighbours.

Under the leadership of Cordell Hull, Secretary of
State in the Roosevelt Administration, and with the
support of the Mackenzie King Administration in
Canada, an assault on the rising tide of protectionism
was begun by the United States in the late 1930's,
through the Reciprocal Trade Agreements Acts.
The Hull crusade for freer trade was distinguished
by its almost fanatical attachment to the most-
favoured-nation principle and the principle of non-
discrimination, and as already mentioned, this view
of the proper standards for commercial policy relations among nations had a strong influence on planning for post-war reconstruction in the international
trade area.

The planners for post-war reconstruction of the
international trading system were faced with something of a dilemma, which was sharpened by differ-

ences among the major countries in their experiences in the 1930's and their resulting conceptions of what the most important problems were. On the one hand, both the pre-1930's conventions of international economic relations and the chaotic constriction of trade in the 1930's, as well as the teachings of classical trade theory, indicated the general desirability of freer, and especially of non-discriminatory, international trading relations. At the same time, the experience of the 1930's showed that the principle of non-discrimination, to be effective, would have to extend far beyond the most-favoured-nation principle into the control of other forms of government intervention in international trade. On the other hand, the experience of the 1930's indicated the necessity for countries in severe balance-of-payments difficulties to be free to resort to forms of restriction of imports other than tariffs, and the possibility that discriminatory trade interventions might in some circumstances have some merits. Furthermore, the changes in the objectives and methods of national economic policy that had occurred as a result of the 1930's and the exigencies of war-time economic management had greatly broadened the range of possible institutional arrangements with which the planners had to be concerned, and had in particular introduced the possibility of a great variety of government controls over, and forms of management of, international trade.

The result of these conflicting influences and considerations, and of the balancing of national influence in the negotiations, was that planning for

D

post-war reconstruction in the area of international
trade was based on two general notions: non-
discrimination as a basic principle of good international behaviour in commercial policy—and much
effort was devoted to defining what this principle
meant in the context of intergovernmental trade
arrangements and governmental control of trade; and
a gradual reduction of barriers to international trade
—especially of non-tariff barriers—by intergovernmental negotiations as a desirable long-run goal. At
the same time it was recognized that countries with
serious balance-of-payments deficits should be
allowed, subject to international supervision, to em-
ploy temporary restrictions on imports, and that in
certain circumstances discriminatory trading arrangements might be beneficial both to the countries concerned and to the world as a whole.

The abortive scheme for an International Trade
Organization belongs to a now-dead era of policy
debate; rather than pursue the details of that debate,
we proceed directly to describe and discuss the main
features of the institution that effectively took its
place, the General Agreement on Tariffs and Trade.
GATT comprises both a set of general principles
for the conduct of international trade, and a series
of rules and conventions governing the relations
among parties to the Agreement with respect to their
commercial policies. To take the latter first, GATT
establishes the rule of law and consultation in international trading relations: one basic principle is
that the relations of the parties to one another should
be embodied in binding legal instruments, the inter-

pretation of which generates a body of rules and precedents for the resolution of conflicts; another is that any actual or proposed policy change by a party to the Agreement should occasion consultation aimed at avoiding or minimizing damage to the trading interests of other contracting parties; a third is that members pledge themselves to work steadily towards the reduction of barriers to international trade, through negotiation within the GATT framework.

As regards the principles of international trade, the central one is the principle of non-discrimination. The contracting parties oblige themselves to extend most-favoured-nation treatment to one another; they also oblige themselves to reduce existing preferential arrangements gradually, through negotiation, and ultimately to eliminate them, and to introduce no new preferences. There is, however, an important exception to these obligations, which has proved crucial in subsequent developments: countries are free to establish free trade areas and customs unions. (A free trade area is an arrangement under which member countries impose no barriers to their trade with each other, while each retains its existing tariffs on trade with outside countries; a customs union entails free trade among members and unification of tariff rates applicable to trade with other countries. Under GATT rules, a customs union must not involve increased discrimination against outside countries, though what this means is impossible to define operationally.) A second major principle is that protection to existing industries should be provided exclusively through tariffs, not through other commercial measures, especially not by import quotas.

The two central features of GATT for our purposes are the principle of non-discrimination and the procedure of pursuing freer trade through the negotiation of reciprocal tariff reductions among countries on a most-favoured-nation basis. Each of these has its peculiar features and implications imposing restrictions on the possibility of action, and a knowledge of these is important to understanding subsequent developments.

Consider first the principle of non-discrimination. This appears on the surface to be an eminently equitable principle; but once one looks into it, it turns out to be nothing of the sort. In the first place, non-discrimination among sources of foreign supply of commodities, ensured by the imposition of a tariff on the commodity at the same rate for each supplier, is not the same thing as non-discrimination among foreign countries, since discrimination among foreign countries can be effected in a nominally 'non-discriminatory' fashion by levying tariffs at relatively high or low rates on the commodities of which particular countries are the dominant suppliers. Secondly, the use of protection intentionally discriminates in favour of domestic producers as against foreigners, and so inherently sanctions discrimination on the basis of national domicile: and if it is ethically acceptable to discriminate against foreigners, what is the ethical logic of insisting that they be discriminated against equally, regardless of circumstances, behaviour, or political ties? Non-discrimination, in other words, is a claim for equal rights of nations to entry to the markets of a particular nation, regardless of these other considerations. In the third place, much post-war theoretical exploration has demonstrated that discriminatory trade arrangements can produce better results—in terms of economic welfare—than non-discriminatory arrangements.

In the immediate post-war period a number of writers proved that discriminatory trade restrictions could produce a multilateral balancing of international payments with less aggregate reduction in world trade than non-discriminatory trade restrictions would entail. Subsequently, more profound theorizing has demonstrated that discriminatory tariff reduction might increase efficiency in allocation of world resources more than non-discriminatory tariff reduction. These findings are now recognized to be particular implications of a fundamental principle, known as 'the theorem of second best'; the substance of that principle is that, for any comparison between two situations each of which is characterized by interferences with the efficiency of resource allocation, there are no *a priori* criteria for determining which situation is better from the point of view of economic welfare. A specific implication of this principle is that, if countries discriminate between their national producers and foreign producers, there is no reason to expect that they or the world as a whole will be better off if they discriminate equally against foreign producers of particular products than if they do not. Insistence on non-discrimination may therefore serve to prevent beneficial changes in international trading arrangements.

The principle of non-discrimination is particularly arbitrary when an exception from it is allowed for free trade areas and customs unions, as in GATT; for these arangements involve one hundred per cent. discrimination in favour of other members as against outsiders. The exception was presumably motivated by the notion that since such arrangements have to apply to the majority or all of the products traded, they are likely to constitute on balance a move towards freer international trade, and so to be economically beneficial. This notion, however, is extremely superficial; theoretical analysis of the economic effects of such arrangements shows that the outcome depends on a balancing of their 'trade-creating' and 'trade-diverting' effects; it also indicates some presumption that partial preferential arrangements are more likely to be beneficial than the complete preferences entailed in free trade areas and customs unions.

Let us now consider the procedure of pursuing free trade through bargaining for non-discriminatory tariff reductions among nations. This procedure has several characteristics antithetical to the objective of trade liberalization. In the first place, the nature of the bargain to be struck—an exchange of tariff reductions—inevitably involves the notion of tariff reduction by a country as a sacrifice of national interest to be compensated for with tariff reductions by other countries at the expense of their national interests; in other words, it emphasizes and reinforces the protectionist motive underlying the tariffs to be bargained over. Secondly, in order to be able and willing to participate, a country must have both a sufficiently large and sufficiently protected domestic market to be able to offer significant concessions, and sufficiently competitive exporting industries to be able to benefit by tariff concessions in foreign markets. These requirements place at a disadvantage both countries with already low tariffs and countries of small importance in international trade, as contrasted with important high-tariff countries, and give an incentive to participants to bargain hard over their own tariff reductions to avoid the sacrifice of future capacity to bargain. Thirdly, the principle of non-discrimination in the context of the bargaining process gives a strong incentive to discrimination of another kind, through concentration of bargaining on commodities of which the bargaining countries are the dominant suppliers. Finally, the bargaining principle makes progress towards freer trade dependent on the willingness of the major countries to pursue it, and enables countries reluctant to pursue it to obstruct progress by asserting their willingness to bargain but obstinately raising difficulties at every point of the bargaining process.

In sum, the procedure for working towards freer trade by bargaining depends on the existence of protective policies and their exploitation in the bargaining process; and the fact that the machinery for liberalizing trade can operate only so long as it is not successful in reaching that objective is a paradox that obviously sets limits to the possibilities of trade liberalization by this route. Furthermore, the pro-

cedure automatically tends to confine the benefits of
trade liberalization to the initially high-tariff countries that are nevertheless important in world trade,
unless these countries extend the benefits to the
smaller countries by voluntary acts of generosity.
This characteristic, incidentally, is one of the important, and valid, bases of criticism of GATT by the
less-developed countries, which the GATT Secretariat
has been seeking to mollify by its Action Programme
and the United States by certain provisions in the
Trade Expansion Act, and which underlies some of
the demands of the less-developed countries that will
be discussed in detail in the next Section.

We now turn to the evolution of international
trading arrangements and of GATT in relation to
them. Like the International Monetary Fund with
respect to monetary developments, GATT was
shunted aside by the dollar shortage—which in the
immediate post-war period gave rise to a proliferation
of quantitative and exchange controls on imports in
the Continental European countries and in Britain
—and by the European Recovery Programme, which
sought to restore orderly conditions with the support
of Marshall Aid. Under the pressure of the dollar
shortage, European discrimination against dollar
goods was not merely tolerated but actively encour-
aged. Both the dollar problem and the development
of the cold war led the United States, which was
paying the piper and calling the tune, to give
primary emphasis to the vaguely defined concept of
European economic integration, which in practice
meant giving priority to the liberalization of

restrictions on intra-European trade through the Organization for European Economic Co-operation— the European side of the Marshall Plan—over the liberalization of restrictions on trade in general through GATT.

GATT was established and began to function, and several rounds of trade negotiations were held, which did over the longer run have a significant influence in expanding world trade, though at the time they appeared to be mostly an exchange of genuine tariff reductions by the United States and Canada for empty gestures in the tariff-cutting direction by the European countries. A significant development in the opposite direction, however, was the granting of a waiver sought by the United States which exempted agricultural policies from the rules of GATT; this postponed indefinitely the assault on a problem whose seriousness has increased rapidly with the passage of time, and which has become a central issue in contemporary trade negotiations. Moreover, after the first flush of tariff-cutting negotiations, the United States appeared to be losing its enthusiasm for freer trade, with domestic protectionist sentiment rising through the latter fifties; and in any case its capacity to negotiate reciprocal tariff reductions was being bought by the results of past negotiations close to the limits allowed by an increasingly protectionist Congress.

As just mentioned, a major goal of post-war U.S. foreign economic policy in Europe was European economic integration. There were, however, two alternative routes to such integration, both of which were pursued simultaneously and in conflict with one another. One was integration through close economic co-operation and co-ordination of economic policy among the European countries, on the basis of common problems and interests distinguishing them from the rest of the world economy, and within the framework of that world economy; this was the OEEC route, favoured by Britain and the other countries on the periphery of Europe. The other was explicit integration through the merging of national economies in a supra-national economy—the common market route, which was initiated by the formation of the European Coal and Steel Community among the six central Continental nations and has since evolved as the European Economic Community. The former route was consistent with a gradual progression towards reconstruction of the kind of world economy envisaged by post-war economic planning; the latter entailed a radical change in the structure of the world economy and the balance of power in it, through the creation of a European economic *bloc,* which many of its proponents supported mainly as a preliminary to a European political union that would constitute a political power comparable to the United States and Russia.

The conflict between the two approaches to European integration emerged into the open with a proposal advanced in 1955 to enlarge the common market in coal and steel into a comprehensive common market among the six member countries. (A common market involves not only a customs union but the elimination of barriers to the free movement of labour and capital and the harmonization of tax-

ation and other legislation affecting international
competition, together with the adoption of a common agricultural policy and the creation of various
supra-national institutions of economic policy formation and administration.) The other European
countries, led by Britain, proposed the formation of
a European Free Trade Area in industrial products,
within which the Common Market would be included. This proposal, while primarily prompted by
a self-interested desire to avoid the political and the
more exacting economic commitments of the Common Market and to retain freedom of action with
respect to outside countries, was also motivated by
some sense of responsibility towards preserving a
liberal international economic system. There was a
protracted process of investigation and negotiation,
in which the French deployed with masterly skill a
talent for raising unexpected difficulties while
keeping their partners bargaining hopefully until the
bitter French-determined end—a talent exercised
subsequently in keeping the British out of the Common Market, and to all appearances exercised again
to frustrate the intentions of the Kennedy Round.
In the end, the proposal for a European Free Trade
Area was rejected by the French, and the European
Economic Community of the Six was established as
planned. The outer seven European countries then
proceeded to establish a European Free Trade Association among themselves, with the obvious intention
of resuming negotiations at a later date.

In the course of these negotiations, an important
role was played behind the scenes by United States

foreign economic policy; for the attachment of the
United States to the notion of European integration
led that country to favour the project for a Common
Market and to oppose the looser arrangement of a
Free Trade Area. Without this receptive attitude on
the part of the United States it is extremely doubtful
whether the Six could have been successful in establishing the Common Market in its present form,
especially as the consistency of some of its arrangements with the principles of GATT is open to
serious question. (The same attitude, incidentally,
led the United States later to encourage and support
Britain's application for entry to the Common Market, which support was partly responsible for the
ultimate rejection of Britain's application.) It is one
of the major ironies of post-war economic policy history that the United States should have devoted so
much effort to the creation of a European super-
economy, whose existence and policies now constitute
the most serious threat to the attainment of the
foreign economic (and military) policy objectives the
United States intended to serve by creating it. The
obvious analogy with the tale of Frankenstein's mon-
ster requires no elaboration.

While these negotiations concerning the Free Trade
Area proposal were proceeding, and the Common
Market was approaching its inaugural date of 1
January 1959, the United States balance of payments
was moving into the position of substantial chronic
deficit that has characterized the years since 1957.
The emergence of a U.S. balance-of-payments prob-
lem, and the increasingly apparent intransigence of

this problem, forced sharply on the United States an awareness of the adverse implications for its international payments position of the implementation of the Common Market Treaty, implications which had been considered and dismissed as of secondary importance during the comfortable period of chronic dollar shortage. The formation of the Common Market threatened the U.S. balance-of-payments position in two ways—directly, through tariff discrimination against U.S. exports, and indirectly, through the attractions of a booming protected European market to U.S. direct and portfolio investment.

With respect to the direct threat to exports, a particularly acute source of concern was the common agricultural policy that formed the counterpart of internal free trade in industrial products in the Common Market arrangements. This policy envisaged a common level of supported prices for major agricultural products throughout the Common Market, reinforced by a system of variable levies on imports designed to raise the prices of imported supplies above the supported internal price level and so provide internal producers with as large a share of the market as they could supply, regardless of the prices at which external supplies were available, together with arrangements for subsidized disposal of any resulting surpluses in the world market.

This policy is in its broad outlines the same as the agricultural policy long pursued in the United States, and for which the U.S. had earlier obtained a GATT waiver. It is occasioned by the same fundamental forces as have dictated U.S. agricultural policy: the rapid increase in agricultural productivity due to mechanization, fertilization, and scientific management, in the face of inelastic demands for farm produce; the inability of farm people to move off the land into industry rapidly enough for the incomes of those still on the land to remain comparable to the incomes of urban-dwelling industrial workers; and the political power of the farmers to exact assistance in the form of high prices for their produce, in lieu of the economically rational but politically uncontemplatable remedy of accelerating their migration from agriculture into industry. The only difference between the situations of Europe and the United States is that the United States is a major net exporter of agricultural products, whereas Europe has been a net importer and the United States's most important commercial customer—though that situation is changing rapidly with the progress of the agricultural revolution in Europe.

The United States discovered that it had a vital interest in the levels at which the Common Market support prices for agricultural products were fixed, since these would determine both the extent of its losses of established European markets for agricultural products and the extent to which Europe would eventually appear as a rival purveyor of subsidized agricultural exports in the world market. In attempting to argue this interest, however, the United States has been hoist with its own petard, since it own past insistence on autonomy of domestic agricultural policy has provided a precedent for European insistence on the same autonomy.

The level of European agricultural support prices has also been a vital matter to the members of the Common Market, and in particular a bone of contention between Germany and France, since French agriculture is more efficient and lower-cost than German agriculture. Fixing of the support prices at a low level would have involved expansion of French agricultural sales to Germany, benefiting German consumers but undermining German agricultural incomes and facing Germany with a serious farm problem; fixing of the support prices at a high level would have enabled German agriculture to survive as at present organized, but induced French agriculture to produce large surpluses, creating a serious surplus disposal problem for France. French insistence on low prices, and German unwillingness to sacrifice the German farm interest to this insistence, prevented the issue from being settled before the Kennedy Round of GATT negotiations officially began, in spite of American declarations that negotiations could not begin without its being settled, and at one time the issue seemed to threaten a dissolution of the Common Market. The issue has, however, subsquently been settled on the lines stipulated by the French, the settlement being reached with the help of an agreement to make substantial payments to Germany and Italy in compensation for the resulting losses to their farmers.

In addition to its balance-of-payments reasons for concern about the effects of the unfolding of the Common Market Treaty, the United States has had other and more altruistic reasons for concern. One arises from the threat that, contrary to the whole intent of its support of European economic integration and of its post-war foreign economic policy, the Common Market will become a highly protective economic *bloc* pursuing discriminatory policies in its trade relations with the rest of the world, thus recreating the conditions of the 1930's which it was the purpose of post-war economic planning to remedy. Another stems from the growing involvement of the United States in the problems of the less-developed countries, and especially of Latin America, and pertains to the adverse effects on the interests of the less-developed countries of a variety of protective features of the Common Market, and particularly of the discrimination against other less-developed countries inherent in the free access to the European market allowed to the former colonies and dependencies that have been granted Associate status in the Common Market. Finally, the United States has been concerned about preserving the unity of the Atlantic Alliance, and with the effects on it of the emergence of the Common Market countries as a rival economic and military force in world affairs.

The outcome of these concerns and considerations was a bold decision by the United States, inspired by President Kennedy, to draw the sting of the Common Market by giving the President vastly enlarged new powers to negotiate reciprocal tariff reductions with the Common Market, in the confident expectation that the Common Market countries would jump at the chance to exchange massive tariff concessions with the United States. The decision was embodied in the Trade Expansion Act of 1962, which was 'sold' to Congress and the American people largely on grounds of its political necessity to the preservation of the Atlantic Alliance, together with some doubtful argument to the effect that reciprocal tariff reduction would improve the U.S. balance of payments, and an appeal to American free enterprise to show the courage of its convictions. The Act involved a variety of departures from traditional U.S. tariff legislation too numerous to be recounted here, of which the most notable were the provision for across-the-board tariff cuts to be phased over a period of five years, the inclusion of agricultural policy in the negotiations, and the supplementation and intended replacement of the traditional escape clause procedures by provision for adjustment assistance to domestic industries injured by increased imports resulting from tariff reductions. The main provisions of the Act permitted negotiation of tariff cuts up to one hundred per cent. on commodity groups in which exports by the United States and the Common Market countries accounted for 80 per cent. or more of free-world trade (the 'dominant supplier' authority); tariff cuts of up to 50 per cent. on other commodities; elimination of U.S. tariffs of 5 per cent. and under; elimination of tariffs on tropical agricultural and forest products, conditional on the Common Market's doing the same; and negotiation on agricultural policy and on non-tariff barriers to trade.

The lynch-pin of the legislation was the dominant supplier authority, which was cleverly designed with two ends in view—to preserve the principle of non-

E

discrimination while violating its spirit, so as to allow the deepest tariff cuts to be concentrated on commodities of bilateral interest to the United States and the Common Market; and to assist the U.S. balance of payments, since it was thought that the United States's technological leadership in the commodities in question and the slackness of its economy would permit it to expand its exports more rapidly than could Europe, where the labour market was much tighter. Other features of the legislation were designed to permit the United States to negotiate tariff reductions with Europe that would unilaterally benefit the less-developed countries, whose complaints against GATT as a 'rich man's club' had already become vociferous.

The dominant supplier authority was, however, predicated on the expectation that Britain would be admitted to membership in the Common Market, as the 'Grand Design' of President Kennedy's policy towards Europe intended her to be. France's rejection of Britain's application for membership in the Common Market knocked the lynch-pin out of the Trade Expansion Act, by reducing the eligible commodity groups from perhaps twenty-five to two (depending on the interpretation)—vegetable oils and aircraft, neither of which offers scope for a vast liberalization of trade, vegetable oils being an agricultural product and aircraft transactions being heavily controlled by government policy.

The United States was therefore obliged to embark on the Kennedy Round on the basis of the 50 per cent. general authority for tariff-cutting. It did so in the expectation that a cut of this magnitude would be sufficient to induce the Common Market countries to respond eagerly, and particularly to be willing to exchange concessions on their agricultural support prices and tariffs for reductions in U.S. tariffs on industrial products. This has not proved to be the case. The Common Market countries have stood firm on their autonomy in agricultural policy, and, as mentioned, have forced the United States to give way on its insistence that the Common Market support prices for agricultural products had to be determined before the Kennedy Round could begin. Equally important, the Common Market countries, primarily at the instigation of the French, have raised a series of objections to the equity and appropriateness of a 50 per cent. reciprocal reduction in tariffs.

At the beginning of the preparations for the Kennedy Round, early in 1963, the French pressed the view that the objective of negotiations should be, not an equal percentage reduction of tariff rates, but a rationalization of tariff structures around lower rates, 'rationality' consisting of a low rate generally applicable to raw materials, a higher rate generally applicable to semi-manufactured goods, and a still higher rate generally applicable to finished manufactures. Whether such a tariff structure is really rational is a debatable question, since what matters for 'rationality' is the 'effective' rate of protection of value added, which depends on the ratio of value added to the values of inputs of semi-manufactures and raw materials, as well as on the rates in the tariff

structure.[1] Subsequently, the French made an issue
of the fact that U.S. tariff rates, though they average
somewhat higher or lower than Common Market
tariff rates, depending on what average is used, vary
substantially more from item to item, and claimed
that equal percentage reductions in these rates would
be unfair to the Common Market. This is the so-
called 'tariff disparity issue'.[2] It can be shown mathe-
matically that the country with the greater dispersion
of tariff rates does tend to obtain the greater increase
in trade from equal percentage tariff cuts, the average
tariff rate, initial trade volume, and elasticity of import demand being the same, though the advantage
is rather slight.[3]

The tariff disparity issue, however, soon shifted to
concern about disparities between tariff rates levied
by different countries on the same commodity, and
a claim that the lower-tariff country should not have
to cut its tariff by as much as the high-tariff country.
The French argument on this score rested on the
contention that high tariff rates contain a great deal
of 'water'—i.e., unnecessary protection—and the
theory that high tariffs yield excess profits that can
be used unfairly to subsidize exports. After long
argument, the U.S. negotiators concluded that

1. For a detailed analysis of this point, see Harry G. Johnson,
"The Theory of Tariff Structure, With Special Reference to World
Trade and Development", in Harry G. Johnson and Peter B.
Kenen, *Trade and Development*, Etudes et Travaux de l'Institut
Universitaire de Hautes Etudes Internationales (Geneva: Librairie
Droz, 1965); see also pp. 84–7 below.
2. For a full analysis of this issue, see Richard N. Cooper, "Tariff
Dispersion and Trade Negotiations", *Journal of Political Economy*,
LXXII, no. 6 (December 1964), 597–603.

yielding to the French claim would have little effect on U.S. exports, since they believed that the high tariff rates contained little water, and that commodities that required high protection would be unlikely to be exportable whatever the tariff concession they received. A compromise formula was arrived at, according to which a disparity was defined as a tariff rate in one country more than double that in the other and above it by ten percentage points; and in

3. Since this point is not obvious, a simple demonstration of it may be useful. Assume a world of two countries A and B, with the same total imports (measured in unit values at world prices) M, same elasticity of demand η for each good imported, and same average tariff rate; but assume that A has a single tariff rate t whereas B has two tariff rates t_1 and t_2, such that $m_1 t_1 + m_2 t_2 = t$, where m_1 and m_2 are the proportions of total imports subject to each tariff, and $m_1 + m_2 = 1$.

By definition, $\qquad \eta = -\dfrac{1+t}{M}\ \dfrac{dM}{d(1+t)} = -\dfrac{1+t}{M}\ \dfrac{dM,}{dt}$

and assuming that imports are in perfectly elastic supply, the effect of a tariff cut of $(-dt)$ on imports is $dM = \dfrac{M\eta}{1+t}(-dt)$.

For equal proportional tariff cuts in A and B of bt, bt_1, and bt_2,

$$dM_A = \eta Mb\ \frac{t}{1+t}$$

$$dM_B = \eta Mb\ \left(\frac{m_1 t_1}{1+t_1} + \frac{m_2 t_2}{1+t_2}\right)$$

$$dM_A - dM_B = \eta Mb\ \left(\frac{t}{1+t} - \frac{m_1 t_1}{1+t_1} - \frac{m_2 t_2}{1+t_2}\right)$$

Using $t = m_1 t_1 + m_2 t_2$, this becomes

$$dM_A - dM_B = \eta Mb\ \left(\frac{m_1 t_1\ (t_1 - t)\ (1+t_2) + m_2 t_2\ (t_2 - t)\ (1+t_1)}{(1+t)\ (1+t_1)\ (1+t_2)}\right)$$

Using $m_1 + m_2 = 1$, $t_1 - t = m_2(t_1 - t_2)$, and $t_2 - t = m_1(t_2 - t_1)$; on substitution into the foregoing formula,

$$dM_A - dM_B = \eta Mbm_1 m_2\ \frac{(t_1 - t_2)^2}{(1+t)\ (1+t_1)\ (1+t_2)}$$

This is necessarily positive, indicating that B's exports to A expand more than B's imports from A.

Note however, that $\dfrac{dM_A - dM_B}{dM_A} = \dfrac{m_1 m_2\ (t_1 - t_2)^2}{t(1+t_1)\ (1+t_2)}$, an expression which by its nature must be a small fraction.

case of such disparity the lower-tariff country is obliged to cut its tariff by only 25 per cent.[4]

Throughout this stage of the negotiations the French continued to express their preference for a tariff cut of less than 50 per cent., but agreement was eventually reached on the principle of bargaining for a 50 per cent. reduction. It is in connection with the prospects for actually achieving a general tariff cut of this magnitude that the agreement reached on the disparities issue acquires its significance, and raises problems about how much will actually be achieved by the conclusion of the Kennedy Round, expected some time in 1965-66. The 50 per cent. cut is a general objective, defining a theoretical maximum cut, and the cut actually achieved may be substantially less. In the first place, each party to the negotiations has the right to except a declared list of commodities from the negotiations, in whole or in part. These lists were deposited on 16 November with the GATT authorities; the exceptions listed by the Common Market covered a significantly higher percentage of the value of imports than did the lists deposited by the United States and Britain, largely because of last-minute pressure by the French, but nevertheless most observers seem to have found the relative brevity of the Common Market list encouraging. Secondly, however, each party is entitled

4. For a more detailed account of this and other issues raised during the preparations for the Kennedy Round, see Robert E. Baldwin, "Tariff-Cutting Techniques in the Kennedy Round", in R. E. Caves, H. G. Johnson, and P. B. Kenen (eds.), *Trade, Growth and the Balance of Payments: Essays in Honor of Gottfried Haberler* (Chicago: Rand McNally, 1965).

to claim disparities on the items not exempted from the negotiations; and this is less innocuous than it might appear, because disparities can be claimed not merely as between the Common Market and the U.S. tariffs, but with respect to the tariffs of any pair of countries.

With the depositing of the lists of exceptions the Kennedy Round of GATT negotiations officially commenced. What are the prospects for its success? 'Success' is, of course, a relative term in this context, and undoubtedly, if any agreement to reduce tariffs emerges, the negotiations will be hailed as a success, since it is only human nature to focus on the difference between the outcome of a bargain and the consequences of no bargain, rather than the difference between the bargain reached and the bargain initially hoped for. The latter difference, however, is analytically the more important one; and from this point of view the Kennedy Round can already be judged to be largely abortive. As already mentioned, the main objective of the Trade Expansion Act—completely free trade in a large sector of industrial products between Europe and the United States—has been frustrated by the rejection of British entry into the Common Market, and the bargaining has instead been concerned with partial tariff reductions of the type achieved through previous rounds of GATT negotiations, albeit on a much grander scale. Little progress, if any, has been made with respect to agricultural policies, which are a problem of vital importance to the whole world, and especially to the less developed countries; nor has much been accomplished with respect to the special deal for the benefit of the less-developed countries that was provided for in the Trade Expansion Act and outlined in the GATT Action Programme. Finally, little attention has been given to the problem of non-tariff barriers to trade, a problem whose importance increases as nations become more ingenious in devising protective devices and as tariff barriers are reduced.

The Kennedy Round has therefore become concentrated on bargaining over a reduction in tariffs on trade in industrial products. What are the prospects for success here? While the agreement on the 50 per cent. reduction target and the depositing of the exception lists seems to promise a substantial success in tariff-cutting, all they really mean is that the final stage of the bargaining process has been reached successfully. Much may happen in the course of 1965 to prevent its completion on the lines initially established: differences in the exceptions list may occasion modifications of the 50 per cent. reduction target for non-excepted goods; disparities claims pressed sufficiently broadly and persistently could reduce the proceedings to a chaos of bargaining on a commodity-by-commodity basis, an exhausting process highly conducive to the end result of an average tariff cut much smaller than the target reduction, as past rounds of GATT have amply demonstrated; finally, it is not beyond the bounds of possibility that the French will find some arbitrary reason for breaking off negotiations by the Common Market at the last moment, as they have previously done with respect to the European Free Trade Area proposal and Britain's application to join the Common Market.

There are therefore good reasons for pessimism about the prospects of the Kennedy Round's arriving at tariff reductions anywhere in the neighbourhood of the 50 per cent. target. If it does not—and, in the broader context of United States policy objectives, even if it does—the effort of the United States to contain the disruptive consequences of the formation of the Common Market within the confines of the general advance towards a multilateral non-discriminatory liberal trading system envisaged by post-war reconstruction will have failed. That failure inevitably implies a tendency towards regionalism rather than multilateralism in world trading arrangements, for there are now two powerful political and economic units in the free world—the European Economic Community and the United States—where formerly there was one; and it has become abundantly clear that they have different concepts of how the international economy should be organized and managed. The rivalry between them is certain to produce some polarization of the rest of the countries of the free world about these two centres of political and economic power.

Public opinion in the United States has already been deeply disappointed by the reluctance of the Common Market countries—and especially the frequent refusal of France—to co-operate in taking actions thought necessary by the United States to strengthen the Atlantic Alliance politically and economically. Moreover, with the assassination of President Kennedy and the succession of President

Johnson, the United States Administration has turned its attention from the international to the domestic field. With the passage of the Trade Expansion Act the United States has in all probability shot its bolt on behalf of non-discriminatory freeing of international trade by negotiation under GATT, at least for the immediately foreseeable future. Disappointment with the outcome of the Kennedy Round —which is likely to be felt even if a reasonable approximation to the target tariff reduction is achieved—is extremely likely to cause the United States to lose interest in the further liberalization of trade, especially in view of the persistence and recent worsening of its chronic balance-of-payments problem. At best, the United States would be likely to abandon its attachment to the principle of non-discrimination —which would, as explained earlier, be no great loss, but rather a step in the direction of economic realism —and to turn its attention in the direction of preferential trading arrangements.[5] Such a tendency has already been demonstrated by the negotiation between the United States and Canada of a scheme for free trade in automotive products;[6] and some

5. Randall Hinshaw argues cogently that if the principle of non-discrimination clashes with the principle of reciprocity in United States foreign economic policy, the United States should choose reciprocity and abandon non-discrimination. See his *The European Community and American Trade: A Study in Atlantic Economics and Policy* (New York: Praeger, 1964), chap. 9.
6. On the Canadian side, the agreement on trade in automotive products is not a free trade scheme but a more efficient scheme for protecting the automotive industries, since free trade applies to producers and not to consumers, and is conditional on the achievement of certain targets for production in Canada.

observers have expressed the expectation that if the European Economic Community proves intransigent in the last stage of the Kennedy Round, the United States's next move will be towards negotiating preferential tariff reduction with the other countries of the Atlantic Community—Canada and the members of the European Free Trade Association. This would, of course, require new negotiating authority for the American Administration, the securing of which from Congress would probably take considerable time.

Freedom of trade, as was argued in Section II, is of great importance for the efficiency of resource allocation and the transmission and diffusion of the process of economic growth in the world economy. From that point of view, the failure of the Kennedy Round to achieve the grand objective intended, and the ensuing prospect of the growth of regionalism in the world economy, is likely to be a serious source of future trouble, not only in relations between the United States, but also, and more economically damagingly, in the relations between the developing and the advanced countries. The problems involved in those relations are the subject of the next (and final) Section.

5.   Problems of Developing Countries

THE plans for post-war reconstruction laid down at Bretton Woods called for and resulted in the establishment of three new international institutions: the International Monetary Fund, designed to provide a stronger and more effective international monetary system by providing international credit facilities to supplement gold, and an internationally-controlled mechanism of adjustment; the General Agreement on Tariffs and Trade, designed to provide an agency for the gradual elimination of non-tariff barriers to trade and of discriminatory trading practices, and the gradual reduction of tariffs through international negotiation on most-favoured-nation lines; and the International Bank for Reconstruction and Development ('World Bank'), designed to provide a steady flow of capital on fair terms to countries needing such capital for their economic development. The two preceding Sections of this survey have traced the evolution of the international economic system and the problems pertaining thereto that have emerged in the post-war period, in the areas of international economic organization for which the first two of the new international institutions were designed to assume responsibility. A major common theme of the exposition has been that in each case the international institution devised with so much thoughtful care at Bretton Woods was pushed aside from the main stream of evolution by the pressure of unforeseen developments, the centre of the stage having come to be occupied by the politics of economic relations between the United States and the Continental European countries.

This Section of the survey is concerned, very broadly, with the area of responsibility assigned at Bretton Woods to the International Bank for Reconstruction and Development, and might well for the sake of symmetry have been entitled 'Financing Economic Development'. Here too the central institution established by the planners for post-war reconstruction has been brushed aside by the march of events, and the centre of the stage has come to be occupied by economic relations between international power groups; in this case first by rivalry between the United States and the Soviet Union, and more recently by increasing tensions between the developing countries as a group on the one side, and the advanced countries as a group on the other. In the unfolding of these tensions the rivalries among the advanced nations—the United States, the Common Market countries, and the Communist *bloc*—have played an important and complicating role. The issues between the advanced and the developing countries have, however, extended into so many areas that, although they could all be related to the general problem of financing economic development, to present them under that title would involve imposing excessive strain on the concept of 'finance'. This Section has therefore been given a less specific title than the two preceding it.

Like its sister institutions in the monetary and

trade areas, the International Bank was designed very much in the light of the problems of the 1930's, and with the intention of forestalling a recurrence of those problems. The archetypical problem situation of the 1930's, in this context, was that of a 'backward' economy—as they were then rather bluntly called—that had borrowed heavily at high interest rates in the New York market to finance social overhead expenditures, related to a process of economic development based on the export of primary products. The economy now found itself abruptly cut off from the supply of fresh capital, and burdened with heavy interest charges on past borrowing, denominated in foreign currency; these a sharp reduction in its export earnings, due to the fall in primary commodity prices induced by the Great Depression, made it extremely painful and sometimes impossible to pay. It is from this widespread experience of the 1930's, incidentally, that many deep-rooted present-day notions about the needs of developing countries were first derived: for example, the strong aversion to dependence on the export of primary products and the strong emphasis placed on the need for policies of industrialization on the one hand, and the insistence that loans for developmental purposes should be furnished on 'soft' terms—low interest rates, long maturities, repayment in local currency, and waivers of payment in case of balance-of-payments difficulties—on the other. And since the severity of the Great Depression can be attributed primarily to a failure of monetary management—particularly to a failure of domestic monetary management on the part of the U.S. Federal Reserve System, and a failure of international monetary management by co-operation among the leading national central banks—the tenacity with which these notions have survived bears witness to the lastingness of the effects of errors of monetary policy and the importance of a well-functioning international monetary system to world efficiency and economic growth.

The IBRD was designed to ameliorate problems of the type described, by providing a stable source of long-term capital for development loans at reasonably low rates of interest, the terms of which could be modified in case of balance-of-payments difficulties. The institution was, however, constructed on extremely conservative lines—inevitably so, given the dominance at Bretton Woods of the countries that would be putting up the money, and the need to establish an institution that would command financial confidence in face of the unhappy record of the immediate past. This has been the source of the Bank's commercial success, and of the increasing confidence in it that has enabled it over the years gradually to extend the range of its activities. On the other hand, its very financial conservativeness has been a source of sustained and increasing dissatisfaction with it on the part of the less-developed countries, and a major reason why they have been so willing to resort to the alternative source of funds for development, the grants and loans increasingly offered by the governments of the leading advanced countries on a bilaterally-negotiated basis.

The International Bank was essentially designed to play a useful major role in a world economy shaped on the lines of the pre-1930's world, a world of slow-but-steady economic growth and diffusion of economic development, in which the smaller nations were kept fairly firmly under control by the political power of the larger ones, and the political dependencies of established states were expected to grow into independent nationhood only slowly, if at all. In such an environment, the Bank would have served to temper the normal rules of hard commercial practice by well-administered leniency. In fact, however, the post-war world environment has been radically altered by two developments: the powerfully contagious appeal of national independence and self-determination, which swept like wildfire through Asia and Africa in the wake of the War and has created a rash of new nations; and the Cold War and jockeying for political position among the leading nations of both camps, which have led the advanced nations to bid for the political support of new nations (or for the continued adherence of dependencies and former dependencies) by the offer of capital for the financing of economic development and other nationalistic aspirations on especially soft terms, or in the form of grants and donations. The result has been that the Bank has increasingly found itself, not in competition with adamantly profit-maximizing and risk-averse private commercial lenders, but in competition with, and overshadowed by, governments anxious to provide capital for political rather than economic returns.

One major consequence of the competition between the governments of the advanced countries in the provision of capital for the development of the less-developed countries has been that the latter have become increasingly restive about the political and economic strings attached to inter-governmental capital transfers, As a result, they have increasingly sought to use their power in the United Nations—which power has grown with experience and the multiplication of their numbers—to press the advanced countries to provide capital for development on the terms they want: that is, in a large and steady flow on the softest possible terms of credit and without political or economic strings. As an integral part of this effort, they have persistently sought to build up the flow of development capital from the advanced countries channelled to themselves through the institutions of the United Nations, as a substitute for both World Bank funds and direct bilateral transfers of capital between governments. Their efforts in this direction have naturally met with resistance from the advanced countries, which have both a political and economic vested interest in the present methods of providing development capital.

The provision of capital for development investment is not, however, the key to the whole, or even a major part, of the problem of promoting economic development, as understanding of that problem has grown with post-war experience of it. And it is to this larger problem that the discussion of this Section is directed, though the exposition will return eventually

F

to the question of capital transfers from advanced to developing countries.

The notion that capital accumulation is the crux of the development problem is firmly embedded in the early post-war literature on the problem of economic development, and was the foundation of early efforts at development planning; it is only gradually being expelled by practical experience of the difficulties of, and many obstacles to, the establishment of a self-sustaining growth process. The notion was derived from two major origins, the intellectual tradition of English classical economics and a misreading of the Soviet experience with economic planning.

Ever since Ricardo's masterly construction of a vastly-oversimplified long-run model of distribution, the English tradition of economic thought has tended to accept implicitly two basic assumptions of English classical economics: that human labour is a homogeneous mass of brute force, and that technological progress is an exogenous influence of limited strength. In consequence, it has placed the emphasis, in its analysis of the mechanism of growth, on the accumulation of capital, to the neglect on the one hand of the contribution of the acquisition of human skills and on the other of the contribution of the application of scientific methods to the improvement of technology and management. The Ricardian influence was particularly strong in Keynes, who in constructing his short-run theory of employment took the quality of the labour force and the state of knowledge—quite legitimately for his purposes—as given; but it so

happened that the Keynesian apparatus—conveni-
ently extended into a long-run model by Harrod's
addition of the capital-output ratio—was the nearest
and most appealing tool to hand for those who turned
from the pre-war unemployment problem to the post-
war development problem.

The Marxian tradition, which took off from the
Ricardian theory and very quickly became fossilized
in dogmatism, also put the accumulation of capital
at the centre of the mechanism of economic growth.
Moreover, the theory seemed to be confirmed empiric-
ally by Soviet economic planning, which exercised a
great hold over the intellectual imagination of the
1930's by virtue of the contrast between the idea of
planning and the reality of capitalist chaos, and
which placed a strong emphasis on investment,
especially in heavy (i.e. producers' goods) industries.
It is only in recent years that economists have pene-
trated the mythology of Soviet growth to appreciate
the important part played in it by a tight labour
market, high rewards to education, and a consequent
universal incentive to self-improvement by the labour
force, together with substantial investment in
scientific research and development.

There was, too, a third element underlying the
early emphasis on the importance of capital accumulation in economic development—the interaction
of humanitarian liberalism among those who
sympathized with the less-developed peoples and of
nationalist feelings and aspirations among the latter.
Both of these bias the analysis of the causes of backwardness towards explanations that do not infringe

on human self-respect, and therefore towards explanations that concentrate on the ownership or non-ownership of property. Lack of capital as an explanation of poverty implies no slur on human dignity, which may even be increased if poverty can be blamed on deprivation of one's rightful due; lack of skill, application, and ingenuity, on the other hand, carries the implication of inferior humanity, and hence is repugnant to liberals and nationalists alike.

Be that as it may, experience with development problems and development planning has amply demonstrated that economic development is not a simple matter of generating enough capital investment. It is a far more complex problem of generating the human skills and knowledge required for working with and managing the capital, and this in turn requires a transformation of the economic, social, legal, and cultural environment. Appreciation of this problem has been reflected in the creation of facilities for pre-investment surveys through the United Nations Fund for Economic Development, the evolution of techniques of manpower planning in underdeveloped countries to complement investment planning, and a growing emphasis on educational and technical assistance to developing countries.

To establish the development process on a self-sustaining basis, then, requires a transformation of the economy and the society, not merely the provision of capital, though capital is a necessary catalyst. As explained in Section II, the process of international competition, even if it is allowed to operate only imperfectly, contains two automatic mechanisms that tend to transmit the process of economic growth from the advanced countries to the undeveloped or developing countries, and so bring about the requisite transformation: the growth of demand for natural resource products, and the growth-induced upward trend in the price of labour in the advanced countries. These mechanisms operate slowly and gradually, however, and their effects can be neutralized or greatly retarded by social resistance or government policy in the undeveloped regions. The rise of nationalism in the underdeveloped regions of the world in recent years has, however, led the countries of these regions to desire a great acceleration in the transmission of the growth process.

Nationalism as a motivation for the acceleration of economic growth is, however, a two-edged weapon. On the one hand, nationalism may be indispensable in motivating old societies in new states to bear the economic costs and absorb the social changes involved in modernization. On the other hand, in a variety of ways nationalist motivations operate to make the inauguration of economic growth extremely inefficient, possibly to the point of ineffectiveness.[1]

In the first place, nationalism derives its values and objectives from rivalry with, and imitation of, other and better-established nations. One result is considerable diversion of economic resources from productive

1. For a fuller discussion of nationalism in relation to economic development, see Harry G. Johnson, "A Theoretical Model of Economic Nationalism in New and Developing States", *Political Science Quarterly*, LXXX, no. 2 (June, 1965), 169–185.

investment in economic development to consumption of the trappings and symbols of nationhood—a large and well-equipped army, an elaborate diplomatic bureaucracy, impressive public buildings, and other constructional monuments to national pride. Another result is the shaping of development investment plans by a desire for the industrial structure considered essential to a large and important nation— a steel industry, an automotive industry—rather than by considerations of maximum profitability of investment in the circumstances of time and place. Secondly, nationalism is strongly inclined to view economic phenomena solely in terms of property ownership and property rights, property here being defined in the broad sense of anything giving rise to a stream of income; thus nationalism universally espouses the transfer of ownership of businesses and of prestige jobs in industry and government to nationals, on the unproven and dangerous assumption that discrimination of some kind rather than incompetence or indisposition accounts for the ownership of the relevant types of property by non-nationals. Nationalism also displays a strong propensity to concentrate economic planning on the establishment of new activities owned or controlled by nationals, rather than on improvement of the efficiency of existing businesses.

Finally—a corollary of these characteristics—in international relations nationalism is prone to discriminate against foreign enterprise and production, implementing this discrimination by policies of import-substitution and hostility to foreign private investment. In this connection nationalism appeals to a double standard of economic ethics, according to which discrimination against nationals or the nation by foreign nations is inequitable and immoral, but discrimination by the nation on behalf of its nationals against foreigners is totally equitable and ethically justified. Indeed, nationalists believe not only that foreigners should approve of being discriminated against, but that they should actively discriminate against themselves in favour of nationals. As will appear later, this double standard—applied as between advanced and developing nations—is the foundation of the developing nations' views on the proper organization of international economic relations between the two groups.

In accordance with the ideas on the causes of economic underdevelopment and the appropriate remedies for it outlined above, policy with respect to economic development of the underdeveloped countries in the 1950's consisted on the advanced-country side primarily in the provision of development capital through grants and concessional loans, and on the underdeveloped-country side in the planning of the investment (predominantly in industrialization and the creation of 'infra-structure') of the capital made available by domestic savings and transfers from the advanced countries. Such investment was heavily oriented towards import-substitution—the creation of domestic facilities for the production of goods formerly imported; this policy emphasis seemed to follow logically from the demonstrated existence of a market for the product and the need to conserve foreign exchange for the purchase of technologically advanced capital goods. In Latin America, in particular, import substitution was made the key to development policy under the influence of Dr. Prebisch, who derived the necessity for import substitution from an alleged long-run tendency of the terms of trade to turn against primary-producing countries, a policy prescription whose logical and empirical foundations have both been questioned by competent scholars.

In the early stages of concern with the promotion of economic development it was confidently expected on both sides that the take-off into self-sustaining growth could be accomplished with the aid of transfers of capital from the advanced countries that would be limited in both magnitude and duration. As time went on it became increasingly clear that this expectation was grossly over-optimistic, and that the promotion of economic development was a far more difficult problem than previously thought, the solution of which would require not only a larger and longer-sustained flow of capital transfers from the developed to the developing countries, but many other changes in policy as well, in both types of country, particularly with respect to international trading relationships. One factor in this evolution was the growth in the number of developing nations, and the rapid rise in the level of their aspirations for economic growth; this was symbolized by the United Nations' nomination of the 1960's as the 'Development Decade', and the fixing as a target for the decade of a rate of economic growth of 5 per cent.

per annum for the developing countries, a target which these countries have already come to consider much too low. The other major factor was the unsatisfactory experience of the results of development planning as initially practised.

The change of emphasis towards investment in human capital and the application of science consequent on this unsatisfactory experience has already been mentioned. Of greater relevance to international economic relations, however, was a growing realization of the limitations on, and adverse consequences of, the policy of fostering development through import-substitution on a national basis. The indiscriminate pursuit of import-substitution in a small market and from a rudimentary base of industrial skill and organizing ability tended to produce enormous inefficiency and waste—which was often reinforced by the ignorance of planners and bureaucrats about the complexity of the input-output relationships of modern industry and the high technological standards it demands. At the same time it largely failed to generate the automatic steady improvement of productivity through managerial and technological innovation characteristic of industry in the advanced economies.

What the policy of import-substitution was up against was the hard fact that efficiency and growth in industrial production demand a market extensive and rich enough to permit the combination of large-scale production (yielding economies of scale) with extreme specialization (permitting the pervasive exploitation of scientific, technological, and managerial

knowledge) and a market competitive enough to com-
pel management and workers alike to strive con-
tinually to improve their efficiency. Protective
policies aimed at import-substitution, by contrast,
confine industry to a market too small to permit the
exploitation of scale economies and modern technology, and by creating monopolistic market positions
seriously weaken the pressures and incentives for
continuous improvement in efficiency. All of this—
including the bureaucratic bungling—is well docu-
mented by historical experience with protection in
more advanced countries.[2]

Realization of these limitations and disadvantages
of import-substitution as a route to economic
development has prompted the vanguard, at least,
among theorists of economic development to empha-
size increasingly the necessity of planning industrial
growth, not in the previous terms of self-sufficiency,
but in terms of integration with the industry of the
developed countries, as a means of raising the technological level and sophistication of industry in the
less-developed countries; and not in the previous
terms of national planning, but in terms of regional
planning, as a means of combining scale economies
with the advantages of international specialization.
This change of emphasis is dramatically exemplified
by the background document for the United Nations
Conference on Trade and Development prepared by

2. For a critique of the "National Policy" of protection in Canada,
   which disputes the conventional historian's view that this policy
   promoted the country's economic growth, see J. H. Dales, "Some
   Historical and Theoretical Comment on Canada's National
   Policies", *Queen's Quarterly*, LXXI, no. 3 (Autumn 1964), 297-316.

Dr. Prebisch, in which he strongly criticizes the 'inward-looking industrialization' of which he was in the past an outstanding proponent, and recommends instead an outward-looking industrialization policy based on expansion of industrial exports to the advanced countries and on preferential regional groupings of less-developed countries.[3]

These new lines of thinking on industrialization policy represent a considerable improvement in economic rationality over the earlier autarchic cast of development theory; but for that very reason they imply a need for reform of the commercial policies and conventions of the developed countries that the older development theory did not, reform which the developing countries have increasingly been pressing the developed countries to undertake. The old 'inward-looking industrialization' was thoroughly consistent with the protectionist philosophy and practice of the developed nations—the Soviet Union as well as the advanced countries of the West—and raised few problems other than that of patience and tolerance within the established procedures of bargaining for reciprocal tariff reductions under GATT. The proposal of regional preferential groupings, however, conflicts openly with the basic GATT principle of non-discrimination. More important, the new interest in exporting industrial products has led the developing nations to recognize, and protest against, the barriers placed in their way by the tariffs

3. Raúl Prebisch, *Towards a New Trade Policy for Development: Report by the Secretary-General of the United Nations Conference on Trade and Development* (New York: United Nations, 1964).

and non-tariff restrictions imposed by the protectionist policies of the developed countries, and by various
commercial practices of private industry in advanced
countries that are alleged to discriminate unfairly
against the development of industrial production for
export in the developing countries.

The practices of private industry are described
here as allegedly discriminatory, because there are
generally good economic reasons why industry in
advanced countries is reluctant to purchase from, or
produce for export in, the less-developed countries,
so that it is difficult to validate charges of discrimination. Moreover, many of the practices criticized are
associated with, and dependent on, protectionism
in the developed countries. The barriers to industrial
exports from the less-developed countries imposed by
protectionist policies in the developed countries,
however, are real and incontrovertible; and in the
author's judgment they are far more severe than the
developing countries themselves have yet fully
realized.

The reason for this lies in a subtlety of tariff
theory first pointed out in the academic literature by
a Canadian economist, Professor Clarence Barber;[4] it
is simply that the protective effect of a tariff schedule

4. Clarence L. Barber, "Canadian Tariff Policy", *Canadian Journal
    of Economics and Political Science*, XXI, no. 4 (November 1955),
    513-30. See also W. M. Corden, "The Tariff", in Alex Hunter
    (ed.), *The Economics of Australian Industry* (Melbourne: Melbourne
    University Press, 1963); William P. Travis, *The Theory of Trade
    and Protection* (Cambridge, Mass.: Harvard University Press, 1964);
    and Harry G. Johnson, "The Theory of Tariff Structure . . .",
    op. cit.

in promoting industrial production is measured, not by the rates of duties levied on the commodities, but by the effective rate of protection of the value added in manufacturing processes.

To explain what this means, suppose that a certain manufacture is subject to a 20 per cent. duty, and that half of the foreign price is the cost of raw materials or components and half is value added in manufacture (the cost of labour and capital used in the manufacturing process); and suppose that these materials and components are admitted free of duty for use in domestic production. The domestic manufacturer can charge $1.20 for a product that would cost a dollar to import; but since he gets his materials free of duty he can charge 70 cents for value added, which would be supplied by the foreign producer for 50 cents; thus the domestic producer enjoys effective protection at the rate of 40 per cent., as contrasted with the nominal rate of 20 per cent. Professor Barber has calculated that the Canadian tariff provides effective protection at roughly double the nominal rate in the tariff schedule; a rather different type of calculation by a graduate student at the University of Chicago, Mr. Giorgio Basevi, indicates that the effective rate of protection afforded by the U.S. tariff schedule is on the average about one-and-a-half times the nominal tariff rate.[5] The excess of the effective over the nominal rate is due to the admission of materials and semi-finished goods

5.   Giorgio Basevi, "The U.S. Tariff Structure: Estimates of Effective Rates of Protection of U.S. Industries and Industrial Labor", forthcoming in the *Review of Economics and Statistics*.

at lower rates than finished goods. This is a characteristic of virtually all major countries' tariff structures; and it has been accentuated by the results of past tariff reductions negotiated under GATT, and by the formation of the Common Market, both of which have tended to increase the degree of the escalation of tariff rates with stage of production that creates heavy protection for manufacture of finished goods. In European practice, effective protection of manufacturing is further increased by basing the tariff on the c.i.f. (landed) value of imports, so that transport costs as well as production costs enter into the magnitude of the barrier to imports of manufactures.

In the author's judgment, the heavy effective protection given to manufacturing by the tariff structures of the advanced countries is a major long-run barrier to the utilization of the low-wage labour of the less-developed countries in the production of manufactured goods for export to the advanced countries' markets. Similiarly, heavy effective protection of the processing of primary products, through free entry of raw products and the imposition of apparently low tariffs on processed products, is a major obstacle to the establishment of processing facilities in, and the development of exports of products in processed form from, these countries. The significance of these barriers is increased by the fact that low wages in less-developed countries are offset in part by low labour quality; and that value added includes capital costs as well as labour costs, which capital costs are likely to be higher in developing than in developed countries, for many different reasons.[6]

The foregoing remarks relate to the emergent concern of development theorists and planners with industrial exports, which has been prompted by experience with the limitations of autarchic economic development. A more urgent and general concern with the export problems of developing countries has been prompted by growing appreciation of the financial requirements of economic development on the scale planned for the Development Decade and after. Even with the maximum feasible resort to import substitution, development on this scale will require a large and rapidly growing volume of imports, particularly of capital equipment, which the developing countries cannot produce for themselves. The forecasts of requirements of foreign exchange to pay for these imports far exceed the sum of projected earnings from exports. The United Nations Secretariat has estimated that the gap between import requirements and export earnings of developing countries could be of the order of $20 billion a year in 1970, on the basis of the growth target of 5 per cent. per annum.[7] More detailed and professional estimates by Dr. Bela Balassa, sponsored by the U.S. Department of State (Agency for International Development), and based on more realistic judgments

6. In the paper cited in the previous note, Basevi argues that it is reasonable to assume international mobility of capital, so that the relevant effective rate of protection is the rate of protection of value added by labour. For the United States tariff, he calculates that the effective rates of protection of value added by labour average between four and five times the nominal tariff rate.

7. Prebisch, op. cit., 5.

of the rates of growth most likely to be achieved in the various countries, put the estimated gap on current account in 1970 at the lower but still large figure of $12 billion.[8] The prospective magnitude of this current account gap, and the unlikelihood of aid from the developing countries sufficing to fill it (together with some aversion on the part of developing countries towards prolonged dependence on aid from the developed countries) has led the developing countries to become increasingly concerned with the possibility of expanding their exports as a means of financing the rate of development at which they aim.

In this connection it is important to realize that aid and trade are not really substitutes in the provision of finance for development. This is a matter on which there is frequently confusion. There are two important differences between them. First, aid provides additional real resources for development, resources supplied by the country giving the aid. Trade does not in and of itself supply additional resources: it is a means of converting domestic resources into foreign exchange, that is, generalized foreign resources. It can, however, provide additional resources for development if exporting increases the real value or purchasing power of domestic resources above what they would otherwise be worth; and this will be the case if the resources would otherwise be employed

8. Bela Balassa, *Trade Prospects for Developing Countries* (Homewood, Ill.: Richard D. Irwin, 1964), 104-5. Dr. Balassa gives alternative figures based on differing assumptions about rates of growth in developed and developing countries; the figure quoted assumes fulfilment of "most likely" growth rates in the former and "target" growth rates in the latter.

in low-productivity occupations such as the subsistence sector characteristic of many underdeveloped countries, or in high-cost import substitution. This difference is obscured by the practice commonly followed in development economics of starting analysis from the foreign-exchange and balance-of-payments—the monetary—aspects of a problem, instead of the real resources side. One important implication of it is that the developing countries are most certain to gain from increased opportunities to export that consist of the opportunity to obtain higher prices for exports, rather than of the opportunity to export larger quantities of exports—especially as their capacity to supply increased exports may be (and is generally believed by them to be) quite inelastic. Whether consciously or subconsciously, realization of this implication is reflected in the nature of the increased opportunities for export earnings that the developing countries have been demanding from the advanced countries, which mainly involve price increases to be secured through commodity agreements and preferences for industrial products in the markets of the developed countries. The second difference between trade and aid is, as already explained, that trade provides an automatic mechanism for the transmission and continued improvement of skill and technological knowledge, whereas aid does not; in addition, the opportunity for profitable exporting is likely to provide an incentive for the accumulation and investment of private capital, both domestic and foreign, thereby promoting a self-sustaining growth process.

G

What are the major obstacles to the expansion of exports by the developing countries? Many of these obstacles, it needs to be pointed out, are of the developing countries' own making. These include the overvaluation of the currency resulting from inflationary development policies pursued in combination with a fixed exchange rate supported by import and exchange controls; the imposition of heavy taxation on primary-product exports through special export taxes or marketing-board surpluses; the cost-raising and inefficiency-creating effects of indiscriminate industrial protection; and the propensity to harass and hamper foreign enterprises, especially to impose demands for self-sufficient domestic operation on branches of large international corporations which depend for their efficiency on international specialization and division of labour within their corporate structure. It is entirely natural, however, that the developing countries should tend to ignore these factors, and find the main explanation in the policies and practices of the developed countries. On this subject they can make an extremely strong case—and have done so.

One aspect of that case has already been discussed: the barriers imposed by the tariff structures of the advanced countries to exports from the developing countries of manufactured exports and of processed primary products. In respect of manufactured products the developing countries also have a legitimate grievance against the propensity of the developed countries to resort to non-tariff barriers, a particular case of which is the agreement arranged through

GATT to control the expansion of exports of cotton textiles from Asian countries. The major attack, however, has been directed against the agricultural policies of the advanced countries, which, as explained in the preceding Section, involve attempting to raise farm incomes by means of support prices fixed well above world market prices, accompanied by controls of one kind or another on imports to ensure the domestic producer priority in the domestic market, and—in the case of the United States and prospectively of the Common Market—disposal of the resulting surpluses in the world market by one form or another of subsidization.

The developing countries capable of producing these agricultural commodities argue, quite correctly, that these policies solve the agricultural problem of the developed countries at the expense of their own export earnings, both by giving a prior claim on the growth of demand—which is in any event slow—to the agriculture of the developed countries, and by depressing the level of world prices of agricultural products. There is, however, a conflict of interest among the developing countries on this point, since important countries among them are food-deficit areas that have benefited greatly from food provided essentially as a gift by the United States under PL 480. This conflict is reconciled in recommendation of the economically impossible principle that surplus food should be given to the hungry poor nations in ways that do not affect world prices. The developing countries also have a traditional complaint about the instability of primary product prices; and a recently

G*

developed grievance against the high excise taxes placed by European countries on certain important tropical products.

The growing concern of the developing countries with their export earnings crystallized in the proposal for the convening of a United Nations Conference on Trade and Development, which took place in Geneva from March to June of 1964. In the meantime, however, recognition of the developing countries' grievances had led the staff and members of GATT to formulate an Action Programme on their behalf to be implemented in the Kennedy Round. This Action Programme, which will not be described in detail here, goes a long way towards meeting the complaints of the developing countries, by offering unilateral concessions from the developed to the developing countries; but, as explained in the preceding Section, it has been virtually submerged in the course of the tortuous negotiations between the Common Market countries and the United States over the precise terms of reference for bargaining in the Kennedy Round. It should also be mentioned that the International Monetary Fund has taken steps towards relieving the developing countries' traditional grievance about the instability of primary product prices, by setting up (early in 1963) a scheme for the provision of compensatory finance to developing countries whose export earnings have fallen abnormally low, though this scheme is considered insufficiently generous by the less-developed countries.

The United Nations Conference on Trade and Development provided a forum for the airing of the grievances of the developing countries against the developed countries and a vehicle for the demonstration and consolidation of their collective political power. For the United States, which arrived for the Conference ill-prepared, and relied for guidance, as it is only too inclined to do, on a few highly moralistic and vaguely defined principles—notably the principle of non-discrimination and the immorality of international price-fixing agreements—together with the assumption that because it knows that its motives are pure other nations will trust its judgment and excuse it from making any firm commitments, the Conference was a traumatic experience. Not only were the Communist *bloc* countries present and actively egging on the developing countries, but the European countries—both Common Market and other—were in important respects more sympathetic than the United States to the developing countries' point of view, while the French—who, as mentioned earlier, are keenly aware of the political aspects of trade relationships, and who regard preferences rather than tariff reduction as the essence of meaningful trade concessions—actively opposed the U.S. point of view. The result was that the United States was virtually isolated as a minority of one, vote after vote endorsing the position of the developing countries by an overwhelming majority, made up of the Afro-Asian and Latin American countries supported by the Communist *bloc,* with the rest of the developed countries abstaining and only a few (generally the U.K. and Canada), and sometimes none, supporting the United States in voting against the motion. This is not to say that the other advanced countries escaped censure. The bilateral trade and aid policies of the Communist *bloc* came in for severe criticism, and the adverse effects of the Common Market on the trade of outsiders were also attacked. However, criticism of the discriminatory effects of preferential treatment of British Commonwealth members and the associated territories in the Common Market was watered down for the sake of unity, and the conflict of interest over this point reconciled in the principle that these preferences should be regarded as temporary and to be replaced by equally advantageous arrangements not discriminatory among the developing countries.

The main outlines of the case elaborated at UNCTAD against the commercial policies and practices of the developed countries have been developed in the earlier argument of this Section; and reasons have been given for believing that case to possess a high degree of validity. The remedies demanded by the developing countries and recommended in the *Final Act* of UNCTAD, however, raise grave doubts concerning both the general principles on which these remedies are based, and their likely effectiveness in solving the export-earnings problem of the developing countries.[9]

Broadly speaking, the international economic philosophy of the developing countries starts from the recognition that the developed countries discriminate against them; but rather than seeking to replace that

9. *Final Act of the United Nations Conference on Trade and Development* (United Nations E/Conf. 46/L. 28, 1964).

discrimination by principles of equitable and efficient international competition, the developing countries seek to have such discrimination preserved but inverted in their favour, through acceptance of the principle that their producers should be included with the domestic producers rather than with the foreign producers in the existing practice of discrimination in favour of domestic as against foreign producers by the developed countries. Concretely, what the developing countries want is, first, international price supports for their primary products, comparable to the price supports provided for domestic agriculture by the United States and the Common Market and justified by essentially the same logic, to be implemented by international commodity agreements; and, secondly, preferences for their manufactured and semi-manufactured products in the markets of the developed countries. These objectives embody the psychology of economic nationalism discussed earlier, and particularly the nationalist notions that foreigners ought to discriminate in favour of nationals, and that without protection nationals cannot survive against foreign competition. This last notion is explicit in the demand for preferential rather than general reduction of the tariffs of the developed countries. They also reflect the point made earlier about the difference between trade and aid, since they concentrate on obtaining higher prices for exports (this too provides a motivation for preferences rather than for general tariff reduction by the developed countries).

So far as the probable effectiveness of the proposed

remedies is concerned, international commodity agreements designed to increase prices raise a host of
administrative and organizational difficulties well
attested by extensive past experience, the relevance
of which the UNCTAD virtually disregarded.
Economically, such agreements are subject to the
fundamental objection that they amount to an extremely cumbersome method of transferring income
from consumers to producers, a method that entails
considerable economic waste through the distortion
of consumption and production decisions by arbit-
rarily high prices, and through the probable necessity
of production restrictions and surplus disposal. In
addition—a point which has been made by Professor
G. L. Reuber[10]—there are not many commodities
for which the long-run demand is sufficiently inelastic
for price-increasing measures to increase total
revenue; and, as American experience with domestic
price supports abundantly demonstrates, price-fixing
is a very inefficient method of providing equitable
incomes for agricultural producers. It would be
economically far more rational to provide income
transfers directly from the rich to the poor countries,
rather than to seek the same effect through the cumbersome and probably ineffective route of international commodity agreements.

Much the same may be said of preferences for the

10.   G. L. Reuber, *Canada's Interest in the Trade Problems of Less-Developed
Countries* (Montreal: The Canadian Trade Committee, The Private
Planning Association of Canada, 1964), 41-45; on the problems
involved in commodity agreements, see also William E. Haviland,
International Commodity Agreements (Montreal: The Canadian Trade
Committee, The Private Planning Association of Canada, 1964).

developing countries' exports in the markets of the developed countries. In the form in which these have been requested—which envisages the developing countries enjoying a small share of the market at the prevailing domestic prices—they too amount to an income transfer to the producers of the developing countries, and a transfer of a kind that is peculiarly irrational economically. For the amount and distribution of the preferences, and their effects in stimulating industrial production in the developing countries, will depend on the tariff rates (and the associated effective rates of protection) of the developed countries and the extent of the preferences given. Efficient allocation of world resources, and efficient economic development, would be better served by general liberalization of trade, with assistance to the developing countries' industry, if required, being provided by a general production subsidy financed by the developed countries. For the developing countries to take full advantage of trade liberalization by the advanced countries, however, it would in many cases be necessary for them to devalue their currencies and modify the tariffs and other restrictions on trade that now make their industries inefficient and uncompetitive; the strains of these adjustments could be compensated by increased development assistance from the advanced countries, and this would be a good investment for the latter to make.

In general, it can be said that the policy changes demanded by the developing countries from the developed countries amount essentially to the provision of larger transfers of real resources disguised in forms that give the outward appearance of respectable earning of foreign exchange but that entail preserving and further complicating the network of governmental interventions in international trade.

In this connection, it may be noted that the recommendations of UNCTAD with respect to the direct provision of development assistance, which subject was considered at the Conference under the heading of financing expanding trade, also boil down to the covert transfer of larger capital sums. This is so because longer credit terms, grace periods, and low or zero interest rates on loans really amount to gifts to the borrower of the present value of the difference between future payments on the concessionary terms arranged and what would have to be paid on commercially arranged borrowings. The developing countries have also demanded that transfers of development capital should not be tied to purchases from the country supplying the capital. This demand is quite reasonable. The fact that such aid is tied is, on the one hand, the consequence of the inability of the communist system to cope with the problem of effective international division of labour; on the other hand, especially in the case of the United States, it is one of the deplorable consequences of the malfunctioning of the international monetary system discussed in Section III. But the demand of the developing countries to institute reverse tying, by obliging the developed countries to accept repayments of capital lent for industrial investment in the form of purchases of the products of the industries so financed, is merely another example of the tendency already noted of the developing countries to accept the methods of protectionism employed by the advanced countries and to seek merely to reverse them in their own favour.

Besides producing a list of general principles and a set of specific recommendations, the UNCTAD has recommended to the United Nations its own continuation as a permanent body, and envisages the holding of another Conference in 1966. It is clear that the developing countries will continue to exert political pressure on the developed countries to yield to their demands, and that the latter, and particularly the United States, will have to yield at least in part to the pressure. The problem that this poses for the future is whether the inevitable and necessary compromise will take the form of a proliferation of special arrangements for transferring income inefficiently to the developing countries, or whether more economically rational solutions consistent with efficiency in allocation and the promotion of economic growth can be worked out. In this connection, it seems eminently desirable for the developed countries—in the interests of the developing countries and themselves alike—to concentrate on distinguishing and solving rationally two separate aspects of the problem of economic development in the less-developed countries. One is the transfer of real resources from rich to poor countries, which is now cluttered up by the mythology of commercial investment intended to be repaid eventually and in the meantime to be rewarded by the payment of interest. It would clarify matters greatly to make these transfers as outright transfers

of income, allocated among the recipients on inter-
nationally-agreed principles of equity. The other is
the establishment of an international trading system
that will permit and stimulate the participation of
the developing countries on fair terms in the general
process of world economic development. There are
three major obstacles to the establishment of such a
system—perhaps one should say to the initiation of
work on its establishment. One is the international
political rivalry among the major developed countries,
which finds one major field for expression in commercial policy. Another is the failure of the free-
enterprise countries to find effective solutions to the
problem of adjustment to the process of economic
change, especially as it affects agricultural producers
and producers in labour-intensive low-skill industries.
This failure underlies the tendency to rely on protectionist policies to cushion the impact of change
on such producers at the expense of foreigners, a tendency which bears especially heavily on the producers
of the low-income countries of the world. The third
is the nationalism of the developing countries themselves, and the policies and attitudes to which it gives
rise, which tend to create strong resistances to the
engagement of those countries in the main stream of
world economic development.

These are problems to the solution of which the
author cannot pretend to have an answer. In any case,
the purpose of this survey has not been to propose
solutions to current problems of international economic organization, but merely to describe and explain
them.

Index

Acceptance centre, and confidence, 15–16.

Adjustment, domestic, problem of, and effects on commercial policy, 14, 54, 100.

Adjustment, international:
ad hoc methods of, 27, 29, 30, 34, 35, 36.
mechanism of, 9.
problem of, 27, 31, 32, 34.
spurious vs. genuine, 34.

Agricultural products:
Common Market support prices for, 53.
exemption of from GATT, 5, 49.
problem of surpluses, 53–54, 91.
protection of, after World War I, 16.

Agricultural protectionism in advanced countries, 16, 53–54, 91.

Aid:
competition in giving, 72–73.
tying of, 98.

Aid vs. trade in development financing, 88–89.

Anglo-Saxon group, 3.

Automotive products, free trade in, between Canada and U.S.A., 66, 66 n.6.

Balassa, B., 87, 88 n.8.

Baldwin, R. E., 62 n.4.

Barber, C. L., 84, 84 n.4.

Bargaining for non-discriminatory tariff reduction, conflict of with trade, liberalization, 46–47.

Basevi, G., 85, 85 n.5, 87 n.6.

Bernstein, E. F., 33, 33 n.3.

Bernstein plan, *see* Bernstein, E.F.

Bilateralism, advantages of, 39–40, 44–46.

Britain:
application to join Common Market, 52.

balance of payments crisis of 1964, 32.
centre of nineteenth century world economy, 14 ff.

British Imperial Preference, 38.

Capital:
concept of, 11.
human, 11.
role in economic development, 11, 74.

Capital, short-term movements of, 21;
impossibility of controlling, 25.

Central bank collaboration:
interwar, 18.
post World War II, and confidence problem, 25–26.

Commercial policy, conventions of, 37 ff, 41.

Common Market:
agricultural policy, 53 ff.
as protective block, 55–56.
attitude to world economic system, 3 ff.
consistency with GATT, 52.
formation, 50.
in UNCTAD, 93.
threat of to U.S. balance of payments, 52–53.
unwillingness of to negotiate trade liberalization, 58–59.

Communist bloc and UNCTAD, 93–94.

Comparative advantage, principle of, 8, 10.

Compensatory finance, 92.

Competition, freedom of:
and diffusion of development, 13.
and international monetary system, 35.

Confidence problem, 17, 25 ff, 31 ff.

Convertibility of European currencies, 1958, 24.

Cooper, R. N., 61 n.2.
Corden, W. M., 84 n.4.
Crossroads, 2.
Currency fund, weaknesses of, 20.
Customs union, 43.

Dales, J. H., 82 n.2.
Deflation and growth, 14.
"Deflationary bias" of the gold standard, 21.
de Gaulle, General, 4, 32.
Deposit centres, 15.
Devaluation, proposal for compensation of, 97.
Developed countries:
   policies of, as obstacles to development, 90 ff.
Developing countries:
   attitudes of, to international institutions, 4 ff, 48, 84 ff.
   emergence of, as a political force, 3, 80.
   policies of, as obstacles to development, 90.
Development assistance recommendations of UNCTAD, 98.
"Development Decade, The",
   financial requirements of, 87–88.
Development policy in the 1950's, 79 ff.
Development problem, two aspects of, 99–100.
Discriminatory trade restrictions, possible superiority of, 39 ff, 44–45.
Dollar as reserve currency, 23 ff.
"Dollar shortage", 22, 39–40, 48, 53.
Dominant supplier authority, 57–58.
Double standard of nationalism, 79, 95.

Economic development:
   diffusion of, 11 ff, 76 ff.
   in nineteenth century, 14 ff.
   insufficiency of capital accumulation for, need for social transformation in, 76.
   process, 11 ff, 76 ff.
   see Development, Developing.
Economies of scale, and development, 11 ff, 81–82.
Effective protection:
   concept of, 84 ff.
   and tariff disparities issue, 59.
Effective protection of manufactures as barrier to diffusion of development, 86.
English classical tradition, 74.
European Coal and Steel Community, 50.
European economic integration, 48 ff.
European Free Trade Area, 51.
European Free Trade Association, 51.
European monetary co-operation, 23.
Exchange rate changes, 21;
   desirability of, 35.
   resistance to, 24.
Export earnings of developing countries:
   need for, 87 ff.
   obstacles to increasing, 90 ff.
   UNCTAD proposals regarding, 94 ff.
Export earnings vs. development aid, 88–89.

Final Act of UNCTAD, 94, 94 n.9.
Floating exchange rates, 28.
France:
   attitude on world economic organization, 4.
   in UNCTAD, 93.
   negotiating tactics, 51.
Free trade areas, 43.
Free trade, case for, 8 ff.
Free trade in automotive products, 66, 66 n.6.
"Fundamental disequilibrium", 21.

GATT:
  Action Programme, 92.
  and effective protection, 86.
  and non-discrimination, 38.
  and regionalism, 83.
  evolution of, 49 ff.
  exemption of free trade areas
    and customs unions, 43 ff.
  intended functions of, 18.
  principles and conventions of,
    42 ff.
  suspicion of, 5.
  see Most-favoured-nation prin-
    ciple, Multilateralism, Non-
    discrimination.
General Arrangements to Borrow,
  1, 29, 30.
Gold exchange standard, 17, 20,
  24;
  three problems of, 25 ff.
Gold standard:
  collapse of, 18.
  deflationary bias of, 21.
  restoration of, 28.
Great Crash, the, 18.
Group of Ten, 30.
Growth, self-sustaining, 76.
Grubel, H. G., 33 n.3, 34 n.4.

Haviland, W. E., 96 n.10.
Hinshaw, R., 66 n.5.
"hot money", 21.
Hull, Cordell, 40.

Immobility and protection, 13.
Import substitution:
  limitations of, 81.
  policy of, 79–80.
Industrialization:
  and economies of scale and
    competition, 81–82.
  policy of, 79.
Infant industry argument for
  protection, 13–14.
Inflation and international disequilibrium, 33.

International Bank for Reconstruction and Development:
  see World Bank.
International Commodity Agreements:
  problems of, 96.
  proposal for, 95.
International imbalances, proposal for long-term loan financing
  of, 35.
International institutions, divisions regarding, 2 ff.
International investment, freedom
  of, 8.
International Monetary Fund:
  compensatory financing of fluc-
    tuations in export earnings
    by, 92.
  defects of design, 22.
  historical background of, 17–18,
    20 ff.
  1964 meetings of, 1, 32.
  proposed transformation into
    world central bank, 34.
International monetary system:
  advantages of a well-function-
    ing, 8–9.
  and development theory, 70–71.
  and tying of aid, 98.
  contribution to development, 13.
  example of nineteenth century,
    15.
  malfunctioning of, 14, 15.
  ultimate purposes of, 35.
International Trade Organization,
  18, 36, 42.
Investment in human capital, 11.

Johnson, H. G., 34 n.4, 61 n.1,
  77 n.1, 84 n.4.

Kennedy Round, 1, 55, 59, 92;
  already largely abortive, 63.
  likely effects of failure of, 65–67.
  possibilities of failure of, 64–65.
  prospects for success of, 64 ff.
Keynes, J. M., 74.

Liberal international economic system:
  desirability of, 8, 97.
  dynamic case for, 10 ff.
  static case for, 8 ff.
Liquidity, international, 9;
  and IMF, 20.
  long-run problem of, 26, 32, 35.

Machlup, F., 25 n.1.
Malkiel, B., 25 n.1.
Marshall Plan, 22, 48.
Marxian tradition, 75.
Migration:
  freedom of, 8.
  restrictions on, 17.
  role in development, 12.
Most-favoured-nation principle, 37–38, 40, 42, 43, 44;
  see Multilateralism, Non-discrimination.
"Multilateral surveillance", 31.
Multilateralism in foreign aid, 73, 98;
  vs. preferences, 5.
  see Most-favoured-nation principle, Non-discrimination.
Multiple currency reserve plan, 33–34.
Myrdal, G., 11.

Nationalism in developing countries, 75, 77 ff;
  and humanitarianism, 75.
  as two-edged weapon to promote growth, 77 ff.
  concern of with property, 78.
  discrimination by, against foreigners, 78–79.
  emulative origin of objectives of, 77.
  in UNCTAD recommendations, 95.
Natural resource products, demand for, 12.

Nineteen-thirties, lessons of, 18;
  and commercial policy, 38–40.
  and development policy, 69–72.
  and the IMF, 20 ff.
Non-discrimination, principle of, 37 ff;
  and U.S. policy, 40, 66.
  defects of, 44 ff.
  in GATT, 43.
  see GATT, Most-favoured-nation principle, Multilateralism.
Non-tariff barriers to trade, 39, 41, 84, 90–91.

Objectives of economic policy, 9, 27, 41.
Organization for European Economic Co-operation, 49, 50.

Perroux, F., 11.
"Pôles de croissance", 11.
Prebisch, Raúl, 3, 80, 82–3, 83 n.3;
  as critic of import substitution, 83.
  as proponent of import substitution, 80.
Preferences for industrial exports of developing countries, demand for, 89, 95;
  alternatives to, 99–100.
  as disguised income transfer, 97–98.
  defects of, 96–97.
Preferential trading arrangements, 39 ff, 43, 45;
  likely superiority of partial over total, 45–46.
Private industry, alleged discriminatory practices of, 84.
Protection, and immobility, 13;
  and the Great Crash, 18.
  and war, 16–17.
  infant industry argument for, 13–14.

Protectionism, and tariff bargaining, 46–48;
  effects of on developing economies, 81 ff.
  in advanced countries, 13.
  in the United States, 49.

Quotas in IMF:
  defects of, 20–21.
  description of, 20.
  1958 increase in, 28–29.
  1964–5 increase in, 31.

Rationality in development policy, 99–100.
Reciprocal Trade Agreements Acts, 40.
Regionalism:
  and economic development, 83.
  future tendency towards in international trade, 65–67.
Remedies for development finance problem as disguised transfers, 97–98.
Reserve currency system, 25 ff, 36;
  deposit *vs.* acceptance basis of, 15–16.
  proposals to strengthen, 28 ff.
Resources for development, aid *vs.* trade, 88–89.
Reuber, G. L., 96, 96 n.10.
Rivalries among advanced countries, 2 ff, 22–23, 26, 30, 32–33, 49 ff, 55 ff, 59 ff, 65, 69, 72, 73, 92, 93, 100.
Roosa, Robert V., 29, 35.
Rostow, W. W., 11.

"Scarce currency clause", 21.
Smoot-Hawley Tariff of 1930, 17.
Soviet economic planning, 74;
  mythology of, 75.
Speculative capital movements, 15–16, 18, 21, 25.
Subsidies to industrial production in developing countries by advanced countries, 97.

Surplus disposal, 54–55, 91;
  conflict of interest among developing countries over, 91.
"Systematic *ad-hoc*-ery", 35.

Tariff bargaining, 5, 46 ff.
"Tariff disparities issue", 60 ff.
Tariffs, principle of intervention by, 37, 43–44;
  advantages of non-tariff intervention in 1930's, 39.
"Theorem of second best", 45.
Trade and development, 8 ff, 76–77, 82–83.
Trade and transfers as separate aspects of development policy, 99–100.
Trade creation and trade diversion, 46.
Trade Expansion Act of 1962, 48, 56–57;
  probable loss of U.S. interest in, 66.
  provisions of, 57–58.
Trade liberalization, objective of, 43–44;
  difficulties of bargaining for, 46 ff.
Trade *vs.* aid in development financing, 88–89.
Travis, W. P., 84 n.4.
Triffin, R., 34, 34 n.4.

United Nations, 6, 73, 80;
  Fund for Economic Development, 76.
United Nations Conference on Trade and Development, 1, 82, 92 ff;
  Final Act, 94, 94 n.9.
United States and the Common Market, 52 ff.
United States and UNCTAD, 93.
United States balance of payments deficit, 28 ff, 52 ff;
  inflationary effects of in Europe, 33.

United States foreign economic policy:
   after World War I, 16–17, 38, 40.
   after World War II, 22, 48–49, 72.
   in recent years, 3, 29, 54 ff, 65–67, 92–94.

Wages and economic development, 12.
World Bank:
   criticisms of, 5.

design of, 70–71.
intended functions of, 19, 68 ff.
1930's background of, 70.
postwar problems of, 72–73.
World central bank, proposal for, 34, 36.
World economic organization, divisions concerning, 2 ff.
World economy:
   interwar disintegration of, 16–18.
   nineteenth century development of, 14 ff.
   reconstruction of, 18–19.